INVITATION TO SERVICE
STORIES FROM COTS

Invitation to Service: Stories from COTS

Copyright © 2008

ISBN 978-0-6151-8253-7

for Mary Isaak
1919 – 2007

TABLE OF CONTENTS

Mary Isaak

"Share the luck."

Background

Mary Isaak co-founded COTS in 1988, with Laure Reichek. A tireless advo-cate for the homeless, Mary died of congestive heart failure at her home in Petaluma on December 22, 2007, at the age of 88.

Born Mary Booth in Eugene, OR, on Oct. 23, 1919, Mary spent much of her childhood on the University of Oregon campus, where her mother headed a women's dormitory. She later earned degrees in music and English at the university.

After college, Mary moved to Berkeley, where she met her future husband, Georg Isaak, a graduate student at the University of California who served in the Merchant Marine during World War II. The couple moved to Petaluma together, bought a 22-acre farm, and raised five children there.

When the economics of the poultry industry turned against the small farmer, Georg Isaak went back to teaching. Mary went to graduate school at Sonoma State University with plans to go into social work, but after taking a job in the field, she realized that there was too much desk time "messing with budgets" and not enough time working with people. So Mary opened a small school on the ranch, which she ran for several years until her children were grown.

In the late 1980s, Mary and Laure Reichek became increasingly concerned about the homeless problem in Petaluma and in 1988 decided to do something about it. "They saw some people sleeping under a bridge and they were moved," Mary's son Tom Isaak explains. "They just rolled up their sleeves."

Mary served on the board of directors of COTS from the time it was founded until her passing, and volunteered in countless positions. In honor of her dedication and service, in 2004, the Board of Directors named COTS' shelter and transitional housing facility for adults without children "The Mary Isaak Center."

Philosophy of Charity and Service

I've been so lucky. I've had enough money and food. I have got five wonderful healthy grown kids. I've got so much: I'm healthy, I don't hurt. I won't even talk about how lucky I am.

I'm not scrambling to put my own life together, so I've got energy to help others. I haven't thought about this, but my own life has gone pretty well. I've been lucky; that's all there is to it, I think. My philosophy is to share the luck.

Thoughts on Volunteering

Well, I just do it for selfish reasons. It gives me something to do. I don't have a job or dependent children, I don't mow the lawn or raise vegetables. I've got to have something to do. I like the people at COTS. And I feel useful when I do this type of work.

I like doing something that doesn't directly come back to me. I don't know how to say it. It doesn't earn you money, it doesn't earn you esteem, you do it for outgoing reasons. It feels good to do something for someone else. That's just the neatest thing in the world, whether you are picking up an injured puppy or doing something with people.

I found myself saying to someone that "I can't stop the war," and there was some connection. Isn't that odd? I felt, "I can't stop the war," but I could give a thousand bucks to COTS. That gave me a feeling of—power's a good word, I guess. Being able to do *something*.

Oh god, I'm just so lucky COTS happened. That it got picked up by the right people in the right way, and became what it's becoming—because it *is* becoming. And it's given meaning to my life.

I'd tell others that "sharing the luck" might feel good to you. There's so much bad stuff going on in the world, anything we can do—*anything*, in any way—must be done. Whatever little tiny area of the world we can touch...

INTRODUCTION: THE NATURE OF SERVICE AND GIVING

John Records
Executive Director of COTS

COTS brings together people from all walks and stations of life. Those without homes and those who are comfortably housed work together. We hail from various races, ages, religions (and lack thereof), sexual orientations, and political perspectives. We come together in service, in giving and in receiving, the highest common denominator of the great wisdom traditions of humankind. In this Introduction, I'll share with you some of what I've learned about service while working at COTS.

Coming to COTS

It was in the autumn of 1990 that I first encountered COTS. I was driving my old Volvo on a rainy, cold night and saw a man huddled at the side of the road, with his thumb out. I don't usually pick up hitchhikers, but the blasting warm air from the heater as the windshield wipers whipped back and forth reminded me of my good fortune. I wanted to share my comfort, so I pulled over and picked him up.

I opened the door and he climbed into the car. We shook hands and traded names. Jim said he needed a ride to the Petaluma Armory, where he hoped to spend the night in the COTS shelter for homeless men and women.

Once a well-to-do contractor, Jim had lost his home, his family, and his business. His lined face and his worn clothes told how hard his life was now. He spoke about living on the street – where to find work, food, and shelter.

Suddenly, I realized that Jim – the homeless person – was trying to instruct and help me – the middle class, employed person to whom such a thing as being homeless was unthinkable. But Jim knew that anyone can lose their home, and that many are just a paycheck away from the street. So he told me what to do if the unthinkable should ever happen.

As Jim left the car at the Armory, I pondered his kindness and decided to follow him into the Armory and learn more about COTS. I watched him as he spoke with the man at the check-in table.

"Can I get some dinner?"

"Gee, you're too late. We ate at the church tonight."

Jim's face fell. A withered man, sitting on a bench nearby, reached into his shirt pocket.

"Hey! I've got a hard-boiled egg you can have. How 'bout that?"

An egg. The carefully saved egg was a meal for a man who couldn't be sure he'd have enough to eat tomorrow. That egg was his savings account, his pension. It was all of his wealth. Never had I given anything as valuable as that egg. The egg man's gift and service to his fellow human being inspired me to want to contribute to COTS somehow; he brought me to COTS as a volunteer in 1990, and I became Executive Director in 1992. (The above story appeared originally in the *Argus Courier* in June 1992).

Fifteen years later, I continue to serve at COTS and have had the opportunity to observe and support thousands of homeless people as they rebuild their lives, and to work with hundreds of staff members and volunteers.

I've noticed that many people, and not just those who are homeless, often feel lonely, lost, and unloved. When we're hurting, we often don't think straight, and we may make unwise choices that cause additional pain for ourselves and others. But there are almost always avenues available to soothe our suffering, and to facilitate the development of our strongest, best selves. In my experience, service is one of the easiest. This book is part of my exploration of the impact and benefits of service.

One Word is Whispered

I love parables and stories from different times and traditions—they are a painless way to gain insight. Here is one of my favorite little stories. For every soul, there is an angel. The angel works with the soul before it is ready to take embodiment, before it is ready to be born into life on earth. The angel talks with the soul about what to expect from life, and how to be ready for life on earth. And then, just before the soul is ready to be born, its angel whispers one word into its ear: *Give.*

In this one word, our angel tells us all we really need to know. Implicit in the angel's directive, *give*, is a way to heal the fragmentation of our lives, and to establish wholeness.

Service is one expression of this *giving*. To give freely of ourselves, without regard to our own benefit, is service.

What's In It For Me?

Only a life lived for others is worth living.
    —Albert Einstein

Have you ever seen somebody wearing a bracelet with the letters "WWJD?" on it? Some of my Christian friends wear these bracelets. The letters stand for What Would Jesus Do? The idea is for the wearers of the bracelet to be reminded of Jesus, and of how Jesus would behave and make choices, so that they can walk in his footsteps. I like this. I think that most of us could use a reminder of the high standard of behavior which, ideally, we would love to emulate. Now and then I, like many people, seem to be wearing an invisible bracelet that has on it the letters "WIIFM?" In other words, What's In It for Me?

Such a bracelet need not be visible because the letters might as well be branded on our foreheads! There are so many reminders of this imperative in our culture. This message is so relentlessly put forth, we don't really have to work very hard to live this way. It's as if our angel, instead of whispering

Give into our ear just before our birth, decided to shout *Grab!* Perhaps there is a good evolutionary reason for our grabbiness; maybe we have a better chance of surviving and reproducing, thus passing on our genes, if our mandate is to grab. But a life of grabbing isn't conducive to making us happy.

And there's another problem: we can only grab so much, and then our hands get full. If we live a life based on What's In It for Me? we can be temporarily sated, our cup can runneth over with all the material things that are available to us, but we will not be truly satisfied.

I think it was the birth of my children, and the need to curb my own wants in order to meet their needs, that began to crack the hard shell of my selfishness. That shell was shattered when, in the early 80s, the Reagan administration asserted that the U.S. could fight and win a global nuclear war. I felt that my dear ones, my beloved little girls, were in grave danger. In other words, I cared more for something, someone, outside myself than I did for my own wants and needs, and I did all that I could to protect them. This included leaving my job for a year and, with my wife and daughters, engaging in a very challenging trek across the United States with thousands of others to educate the public about nuclear war and disarmament.

Once the hard armor of my selfishness was broken, a life based on giving and good intentions for others gradually grew. This growth has been supported by spiritual reading and the practice of meditation, prayer, and allied disciplines, and by the easy path of service to others.

The Power of Grace

Usually when we are engaged in service we don't think about what's going on at a deeper level. We are probably immersed in the needs of the moment, whether it be talking to a client, reading to a child, or feeding a hungry person. We are simply involved in the act, and that's a good thing; it's better that we are not self-conscious, analyzing our motivation and our response as we do these things.

But nonetheless, something is happening on a deeper level. People invariably say that they feel good when they render service (and by this I mean selfless service, in which we help to meet the need of another without seeking what's in it for us).

I think I know why we feel good when we offer selfless service. Would you kindly bear with me as I try to talk about something of great importance in a way that will make sense to people of varying beliefs and perspectives?

Suppose, for the sake of discussion, that there is a force of kindness and compassion that naturally responds, *through us*, to those in need. I call this force, this elemental flow, *grace*; please use whatever words you like.

For the most part, we live unaware that we can offer ourselves as instruments for the expression of grace. But when we make ourselves available to grace, when we act in accordance with the promptings of grace, we feel good. The action of grace in the world manifests as service to those in need, which is encouraged by all the great wisdom traditions. For example, Jesus tells us that He is present when we feed the hungry, give a drink to the thirsty, when a stranger is received into our homes, when we clothe the naked, when we take care of the sick.

Service graces the giver as well. In St. Francis' famous prayer, he states, "It is in giving that we receive." It is not "in grabbing that we receive!" As I noted earlier, there is only so much that we can hold by grabbing. But by giving, we keep making room for more receiving. Moreover, our capacity to give, and hence what we receive, increases with practice.

If we let our hearts open to the need of another being (or the needs of a situation), that will itself tell us what we must do, and how we must serve. For example, if our baby is crying we can decide to change the baby's diaper with love for our little one rather than with resentment over the task. By this simple change of attitude, responding to the baby's cry with love, we let grace act through us.

The Crucial Ingredient, and Its Byproducts

For most kinds of service we can imagine, a machine could perform the task. For example, a vending machine can provide hot stew to a customer. But a crucial ingredient is missing, and that ingredient is, of course, love.

The Talmud says, "The whole worth of a kind deed is the love that inspires it." This underscores that service of the kind discussed in this book is not merely a mechanical act. Rather, as Sarah Patton Boyle, a U.S. civil rights activist, said, "Service...is love in action, love made flesh; service is the body, the incarnation of love. Love is the impetus, service the act, and creativity the result with many byproducts."

When Patton Boyle says, "Love is the impetus," he is describing the ever-present invitation of grace. The pull of love, its call to us, can take many forms: a sense of connection with someone in need, the inspiration to give something we have just because somebody else might need it, the desire to help someone who's in a situation that sparks a memory of some old pain or loss of our own. The "many byproducts" Ms. Boyle mentions are diverse and unpredictable; they range from a warm glowing feeling in the giver and receiver to the utter transformation of either or both, and perhaps even of those around them.

Inescapable Wounds, Indispensable Joys

A young friend said to me, "I'm trying to figure out what to do with my life. Do you have any thoughts on this?" I pondered as we walked through a beautiful park. Knowing that my friend pushes herself pretty hard, I said, "Well, I'd give a different answer to a different person. But my answer to you is the first thing to do is to give yourself permission to have fun."

"But I can't do that," she said, "when the world is in such trouble. People are starving. A war is looming. And women and children are being abused every day. How can you tell me to have a good time?"

"I just want you to be able to enjoy yourself," I said, "even though there is a lot of pain in the world. We've both seen grim, desperate, fearful activists who feel driven and angry, and who are doing their level best to save something that they see as hanging by a thread. I myself have been like that. I don't know how effective we really are when we're coming from that place. We're running on a corrosive fuel that doesn't feed us and that in fact eats away at us and those around us."

I continued, "I'm not putting people like that down--they have the guts to confront what they see is wrong. And it's true that terrible things are always going on. But it's also true that there is always cause for joy and for celebration. We have to find some kind of accommodation between the woundedness and the joyousness of our world. I think that to the extent our engagement with the woundedness of the world can come from our joy and strength, we will be more effective than if we come from the place of desperation and fear."

I concluded by urging her to root herself in what she finds to be true, good, and loving, to have a positive vision of the future, and to engage the world from that place. The balancing act between the wonder and woundedness of our world is expressed beautifully by the women's singing group Libana in its song, "Be Like a Bird," based on Victor Hugo's "Wings." As Libana puts it:

Be like a bird, who pausing in her flight
on a limb too slight, feels it give way beneath her,
yet sings, sings, knowing she has wings;
yet sings, sings, knowing she has wings.

We can take the risk of alighting on the ever-unreliable branches of the world, engaging with the pain and fragmentation, because we know that our wings will bear us up until we choose to alight again.

If we open ourselves to the woundedness we see in the world, if we accept it as our woundedness too and let our hearts be broken by it so that grace can enter and act through us, we accept the invitation to service. We accept the invitation to participate in the healing of the woundedness of the world, which is our own woundedness as well. This is the healing of ourselves. By the same token, the joy of the world is our own joy, and we can rejoice in the triumphs of others.

I emphasize woundedness more than joyousness because woundedness is more frightening and challenging to connect with. But as grace expresses itself more through us, as we offer ourselves in service to the woundedness of the world, a healing occurs that encompasses us as well as those whom we serve.

For instance, if we are inspired to help a woman who has been abused, that within us which responds to her need is *part of her need*, part of the world's wound which she and we suffer together. The recognition of her suffering, along with the effort and intention to help heal it, are part and parcel of the healing itself. And as her personal healing begins, the universal wound is also addressed.

As a corollary, beginning to heal ourselves, making ourselves more whole, opening ourselves to the gifts of grace, enjoying our lives and expressing and developing our gifts—all this helps to heal the woundedness of the world. Another way to say this is that our individual blossoming and our natural healthy, joyous expression are part of the world's healing.

Immediately in Front of Us

One of the easiest places to offer service is in our families and in our friendships by putting others' needs ahead of our desires. Opportunities to do this may arise at unexpected times.

For example, I had just returned from work and was sitting on the couch reviewing the day's mail. It felt great just to sit down with the mail after a day full of busy meetings. My 18-year-old daughter came to sit by me and I put the mail down, turning my attention to her. "You know, Dad," she said, "I really appreciate it that you're ready for me whenever I'm ready for you. There's never been a time that I needed you that you weren't there for me." In this case, it was a simple, natural thing to drop what I'd been doing in order to be present for my daughter when she needed me. And no award, no honor I've ever received has meant more to me than my daughter's tender thanks.

A Job Is Never Just a Job

"I can't be servile. I give service. There is a difference."
        —Dolores Dante, U.S. waitress
        as quoted in *Working*, book 5, by Studs Terkel (1973)

We can picture "tiers" of service outside the family. Someone might progress from having a regular, off-the-shelf job, to doing such a job with a serviceful attitude, to volunteering now and then in an environment overtly dedicated to service, to having a job that's completely dedicated to service. This has been my own trajectory.

In some ways it's much easier being in a job dedicated to service, because we don't have to struggle to make room for real service and we get a lot of support in living and behaving in a serviceful way. For most of us, full-time employment in a recognized service profession is hard to come by, so our work-a-day job becomes our primary arena for service.

Offering selfless service is possible in any context or environment. Whether we are working in a homeless shelter or in a tech company, whether we are reading to the neighbors' kids or volunteering at the hospice, we can give of ourselves in service to the people and the work at hand.

Sometimes when we are performing selfless service, we encounter difficult and even potentially demeaning situations. We needn't be a doormat as we serve; we needn't be servile. Books and courses are offered on how to deal with difficult people, and I won't dwell on this subject here, except to mention that, in such situations, we must keep in mind the woundedness we all share. When we remember this fundamental reality, we try to be patient with unpleasant or inappropriate behavior and we try to help others regain their balance and perspective, setting boundaries as needed so that we feel our integrity is preserved.

It's important to remember that the woundedness that leads to unpleasant behavior in others is our woundedness too. Even though we may think that we are engaged in an interaction for the purpose of, for example, selling a book as part of our job at the bookstore, the most important service we render on a given day might be to enter into the woundedness of a difficult customer and to give that person needed love and attention.

Rejuvenation and Nourishment

"We make a living by what we get, but we make a life by what we give."
—Winston Churchill

I know many people who live their serviceful attitude in the business world, but they also sometimes seem a little worn out when their work environments are dollar-driven and dehumanizing. They tell me that volunteering with COTS is refreshing and revitalizing. Take for example the viewpoint of Jim Hanson, a real estate broker and former car salesman, who volunteered at COTS for over 10 years:

To me COTS is an oasis. There I can get fulfilled. It's an island in the middle of this turmoil that I can find refuge in. This is real for me and I treasure it. I talk it up all the time. It is an oasis for me. And when I go in there, the staff and volunteers are concerned about me and I'm concerned about them. It's a nice, nice feeling.

As volunteers, we should take small steps and have patience. Look at all the residents, all the people who are homeless, look for that personal pure essence. And have no expectations, none.

If you get involved you'll be happier and you'll be more fulfilled than in anything you've ever done. It won't make you rich in material things, but it'll make you wealthy in friends, relationships and personal well-being. You'll go to bed every night and you'll say, 'That was a good day. That was a cool day today.' You won't have that plaque on the wall for being the outstanding car salesman or whatever, but you'll have it in your head. And you'll sleep well. The inner joy you get is great. You'll find all those other important things will still get done but they won't be as big a deal any more. They're just not that important.

The Corporate Salvage Program

Men and women approaching retirement age should be recycled for public service work, and their companies should foot the bill. We can no longer afford to scrap-pile people.
    —Maggie Kuhn

At COTS, we have developed what I playfully call a "corporate salvage program" for business and professional people, and not just those who are ready to retire. Prior work experience of COTS staff includes management of a billion-dollar corporation, fiscal management in a Fortune 500 company, corporate and real estate law, corporate communications, newspaper reporting, and general administration in tech companies. (Also, some staff come with a background in social services, and others are formerly homeless themselves.)

One of COTS' staff characterized his former job as "maximizing stockholders' equity in the short term." He found it hard to become excited about that. Another staff person, who has worked in government, described his former job as providing the opportunity to "work with people from all walks of life and bring them to their knees, without regard to their race, creed or color," and said that he suffered through the weekends afflicted by "snake-in-the-gut anticipation of inexorable Monday."

While there are ample opportunities in such working environments for selfless service, these environments can be inhospitable. As an alternative, we've created a service-oriented workplace where we can apply the skills and rigor learned in the business world toward COTS' nonprofit mission of providing help and hope to people who are homeless. In doing so, we've demonstrated the truth of the statement that my Civil Procedure professor, Herbert Peterfreund, attributed to the Duchess of Romania: "True happiness comes when we strive with all of our might to do that which must be done." By heeding the call to service, and serving together, we at COTS find both individual and collective happiness and fulfillment.

Beyond Heartbreak

There are many challenges in offering ourselves in service, in offering ourselves into the woundedness of the world. Now and then we encounter something we aren't ready for.

Some years ago in my work at COTS, I met a homeless mother whom I'll call Yvonne, and her 10 year-old daughter whom I'll call Celeste. (These are not their real names.) Yvonne was worn by her years on the street, and there was something about her that reminds me now of a partially-finished cup of old, cold coffee sitting on the counter. She was used up, but not yet disposed of by our uncaring culture.

Yvonne lived with her daughter Celeste in the nooks and crannies of our community, in the homeless shelter when possible, in the back of an old car when she had one, in the bushes when she didn't. Celeste was someone special. At age 10 she was years behind in school (when she had the opportunity to attend), trusting enough to be always ready to laugh, with an expectant sweetness behind her usually hesitant and puzzled eyes.

I had daughters a little younger than Celeste, and that opened me to her. Thinking of their brightness and competence, appreciating how they were ensconced in our happy family life, I sadly watched Celeste at the shelter. Seeing her trusting sweetness and the unlikelihood of her life being a happy one, I reached out to her, and Celeste and I made a deep connection. When I saw her in the shelter, I was able to use my Daddy-of-daughters skills to elicit a special smile from her, letting her know that I knew who she was and that I liked her.

After about a month, it was time for Celeste and Yvonne to leave the shelter, and I lost track of their whereabouts after about a year. Many years later, Celeste and Yvonne appeared again in our community. I was told that Yvonne's boyfriend had been pimping Celeste, selling her on the street.

The image of Celeste as a clouded, innocent child dominated my inner vision and I was torn to pieces. I sobbed, unable to bear the thought of her being repeatedly molested by harsh men, her trust broken again and again and again. In the course of a phone discussion with a clergy member about an unrelated matter, I mentioned my anguish and asked him to pray for me. "Of course," he said. "And wouldn't you like to pray together for her, too?"

I had never thought of that. My response to Celeste's situation was all about me, although it purported to be about her. I was wrapped up in my vicarious agony and somehow it wasn't about Celeste anymore; it was about me and my response to a world in which this could happen to an innocent, and by implication to my own daughters.

Some prospective volunteers have said, "I don't think I could stand to work with the homeless children. It would just break my heart." I can attest from my own experience that this is, indeed, a risk. It's understandable not to want our hearts broken, but when we allow our hearts to break, we also open ourselves to a powerful force that can change our own lives. We realize that we must help. And then we find a way to help.

This is why children in our community have sold lemonade for COTS, given their allowances for the COTS kids, and brought to the shelter their own toys as gifts for the homeless kids. This is why adults have raised funds for COTS by offering beauty treatments, walking classes, and martial arts marathons. This is why people volunteer to serve food, invite homeless families to sleep in their churches, mentor and play with homeless children, and teach classes to homeless adults. This is why the greater COTS community donates 50,000 hours a year of volunteer support for homeless children and adults!

If we don't work with people in need, then who will do it? We really have no alternative but to courageously face the pain in the world, a world in which 50,000 children die daily from preventable causes. We must risk the broken heart, embrace the pain, ask for help, rest when needed, and never give up. To turn away in order to protect our own comfort is to reject the call to participate in the healing of those in need, as well as our own healing, and the world's.

In addition to the risk of heartbreak, to really throw yourself into service is to risk feeling overwhelmed. How can we prevent nuclear war, house all of the homeless, feed all of the hungry, heal all of the sick? If we can't help all of those in need, if we can't cure the problem, then the temptation, the cop-out, is to do nothing. Mother Teresa had good answers for that one: "Never worry about numbers. Help one person at a time, and always start with the person nearest you," and "If you can't feed a hundred people, then feed just one."

Our responsibility is limited. All we have to do is make ourselves available, show up, and do our best. To remind me of this, I've had these signs on the wall of my office:

Full effort is full victory.
　—Gandhi

Don't feel totally, absolutely, overwhelmingly responsible for everything. That's my job.
　—God

Offering service in this spirit, just showing up and doing our best, realizing that the outcome is not in our hands, makes it easy. When it feels hard, when we have feelings of desperation, fear, or even pride, we have temporarily lost our way, closed ourselves to the action of grace through us, and have become focused on ourselves.

When service feels hard and challenging, we can find our way again by opening ourselves to the needs of the people and the situation we're offering service to, thus re-establishing the connection that is part of the healing. We can also engage in other practices that support deep connection, such as meditation and prayer.

Regardless of our religious (or non-religious) orientation, the prayer of St. Francis can be a road map for service. St. Francis implores:

Where there is hatred, let me sow love
Where there is injury, pardon
Where there is doubt, faith
Where there is despair, hope
Where there is darkness, light
Where there is sadness, joy.

St. Francis tells us how to offer ourselves into the woundedness of the world, and how to do it in the most useful way: by entering into the dark and despairing places and giving what is needed, without concern about "What's In It for Me?"

We do this at COTS. We don't offer a theoretical, abstract love, but rather we meet suffering where it lives, and we respond with practical help. Of necessity, the help we provide may sometimes include setting firm boundaries, as well as nurturing, feeding, counseling, educating, training, and sheltering.

If we can face the challenges of service, overcome our fear, dare to love, dare to alight on the branches that we know will give way beneath us, we will share Mother Teresa's experience: "I have found the paradox that if I love until it hurts, then there is no hurt, but only more love."

What we give, we receive: we are healing ourselves as we heal the world and its wounded. This is the secret blessing that comes from offering ourselves in service to homeless children and adults at COTS.

January, 2008

This essay is dedicated, with gratitude, to the egg man.

NOTE FROM THE EDITORIAL AND DESIGN TEAM

When John Records first approached me with this project and I read through these amazing stories and interviews, I felt like the person given the task of releasing a message trapped in a bottle or an important scroll found in a buried chest. Such wonderful thoughts, such inspiring words, and so much time and energy spent thinking about the project, scheduling interviews, conducting interviews, and then more time spent by transcribers charged with the task of getting every word onto paper. But more steps were needed before they could be shared with others.

Our team of editors worked through each interview to capture the spirit of each person, but get their thoughts formatted in a manner that would work for the printed page or website reading. Each interviewee was asked the same series of questions, so we used those to create "landmarks" so that navigating their words would be as simple as possible. We then had another editor review all of the interviews with fresh eyes and work with each interviewee to fill in missing information and obtain approval.

I have always supported COTS, because I believe they accomplish so much to create a better community in Petaluma and Sonoma County and effect real change in people's lives. When you read these interviews, you will gain additional insight about why this organization is so special. Every one of us on the editorial team has learned so much from each of the interviews, and we know that others will, too. It is also interesting to note that the backgrounds and reasons why people enjoy doing this work are as diverse as their philosophies around service and giving.

It has been an honor to give service to COTS by working on this project.

Sara Cummings

Editors: Sara Cummings
                Kristina Flanagan
                Margie Goolan
                Eileen Morris
                Marc Polonsky
                Julie Sykes

Cover Design: Garth Jordan, Sightdesign

Transcribers: Due to an unfortunate computer malfunction, the names of the transcribers were lost. They did an invaluable job and are very much appreciated, and it is unfortunate that we cannot recognize them by name.

I. IT COULD HAPPEN TO ANYONE

I was hungry and you fed me, thirsty and you gave me a drink; I was a stranger and you received me in your homes, naked and you clothed me; I was sick and you took care of me, in prison and you visited me.
　　—Matt. 25:35-36

Homelessness is an economic condition, not a character flaw. The more closely we work with people who are homeless, the more evident it becomes that homelessness could happen to anyone, given the right (or wrong) set of circumstances and events. People who are homeless are not so different from the rest of us.

Those of us who have homes and enjoy the material luxuries of life can count our blessings. We might also remember, when we see homeless people, that "there but for the grace of God go we."

Michelle Baynes

"I believe that God loves everybody the same. I believe in miracles."

Background

Michelle Baynes was born in San Francisco and raised in South San Francisco and Belmont, California before moving to Rohnert Park, California in 1974. Her parents were originally from Utah and Montana; they met at Mission High School in San Francisco. Michelle is divorced and has two sons, John and Richard. She has lived in Petaluma for over 20 years.

A successful Petaluma realtor, Michelle began working at COTS in the early nineties as a volunteer at Children's Haven. Later, Michelle became a member of the COTS staff and performed a wide range of duties including office work, case manager, and overseeing Christmas at the family shelter. Michelle served as Director for the Opportunity Center for over five years and Director for all services for single homeless people. In 2005, Michelle returned to real estate, but she continues to assist her former clients.

Personal Values and Inspiring Role Models

I had a pretty wonderful childhood. There were words my brother, sister, and I couldn't use; for example, we couldn't call each other "stupid" or "dumb." My parents taught us to tell the truth and to respect each other. I would say that we all turned out to be nice people.

Another thing I believe really affected all three of us is that we went through Catechism and Confirmation with the Catholic Church. (My dad was Catholic and my mom was Mormon, although neither of them practiced their faith.) What we learned there helped shape our values, how we treat people, and our spiritual beliefs. It also gave us strength in hard times. I'm not a practicing Catholic but I believe in God and Jesus, and I have a diverse spiritual background.

The lives of Jesus and Mother Teresa influenced me. Although I'm not like Jesus or Mother Teresa, I understand unconditional love, and respect for the value of each life. Also, I remember growing up reading about St. Luke and how he would go to the lepers, and how he would go out on the streets and work with people in need. I valued that.

With COTS, I learned so much from the homeless and other people I met along the way. The experience has strengthened my beliefs.

Discovering Service

When I was a realtor, my colleague Jim Hanson and I were sitting at the computer talking together and I said that I wanted more meaning out of life. I explained that I liked real estate but I really wanted to feel like my life was making some type of difference. And Jim said, *"Oh Michelle, COTS needs volunteers in the Children's Haven, a new program they are starting."* So I came down and started volunteering.

Over the years, my different roles at COTS have helped me with my own growth and self-esteem. Today, I know who I am; I have more self-confidence and don't question myself as much as I used to. I'm more accepting and serene. COTS has helped me with all that.

Things that I thought were so important that aren't important to me today. I see other people differently. I know how to look beyond the surface and see the heart and soul in a human being.

Accepting Challenges and Witnessing Transformations

Among other things, I was a street outreach worker, which was my favorite job. I used to go under bridges and in the camps and talk to people. Even when people wouldn't come back into the shelter, I still had a connection with them. Even if they were staying out and they knew they were dying, there was still that connection; they knew somebody cared about them.

It's really hard when people die on the street. It's terribly sad. When you're out there on the street and literally holding somebody's hand as they say, *"I don't want to die. I don't want to die."* Or when you're watching people continue drinking or staying on the street when they are mentally ill. Some of their pain is caused by the decisions they make; I've accepted this, though it's very hard. They have to choose what they want to do. I still want to be there when they change their mind.

Currently we have a staff member that's been on staff for about a year and a half. I met this person on the street. I watched him for about five years. I met with him, talked to him, and asked about his family. Sometimes he was so sick I thought he was going to die. He was so mired in the disease of alcoholism and drug use that I wondered, "Is this person ever going to stop?" Regardless, I stayed respectful and I would ask him, "What about calling your mom?", or "What about connecting with your family again?" or "Where are you going to be in 10 years? You're young. What's going to happen to you?" He would reply, "I've lost that thing to live for. I've lost hope." We talked about programs, but because of a legal problem he went to jail. I said, "If you get clean, and there's a job available when you come back, we're going to look into that." This person had worked for us twice before but had kind of blown it. Still, the chance to work again kept him going; that was his hope. Also, he called his mom, his dad, and his sister. I think those were lifelines for him too. Eventually, after getting the necessary approval, COTS was able to employ him again. Now, more than a year and a half later, he is a staff member and a gift because of his compassion and his understanding. He's been there. He's blooming, just blooming, because he wanted to change and feel hope.

So connecting with people is important. They have to trust you and you have to let them know how you see them and that you're not judging them. It was a wonderful thing that happened with this person. You see it happen all over COTS. I'd like to see it happen more. I don't think any of us would be able to do the job, or do it for so long, if we weren't effective.

A Life-Changing Story

I was a case manager at the family shelter. A young woman, Nancy, came in with her young son, and I knew she was in an abusive relationship, though she wouldn't admit it. I was worried that she and her son were both being hurt.

Then she told me she had AIDS, and I said, "If I can ever help you in any way . . ." But I already knew what she would ask. She would eventually ask me to take her son, Richard.

Nancy was beaten up a lot. She and Richard got into a battered women's shelter, and I would go with my boyfriend and we would pick Richard up and keep him with us every weekend. And then Nancy said she was going back on the street again, and would I please take care of Richard, and adopt him?

So Richard is my son, and he's been with me since he was six. He's nineteen now.

About Service and Its Rewards

A career in real estate offers more financial rewards, but this isn't about the money. For me, it's about my heart. It's about my spiritual connection with God. It's about how I want to spend my time while I'm on the earth, and what I get back from people. When I go out on the street, I picture God or Jesus going out and meeting with people that other people don't even see. They're invisible to others.

It's a heart connection. The connection is more than saying, *"I have a sleeping bag for you."* It's a connection that builds trust over time. And that person living on the street, sometimes quickly, sometimes years later, if they want help, will come back to you and say, *"I'm ready."*

I get up happy to come to work, even though sometimes I'm tired. Why wouldn't I want to do something that is helping me spiritually and that I believe is God's work?

I don't expect anything back, but I get back so much. In this work, you get back things that are more wonderful than money or anything you could expect. I'm talking about the relationships you have with people. I've learned how to give unconditional love and accept unconditional love in return. I "get back" seeing people changing their lives. It makes my heart feel good. But I don't do this work because of what I'll get in return. I don't want to say, *"If I do this, then I get this back."*

But if I'm out on the street and something happens in the area and it becomes unsafe, I have people backing me. I feel a connection that will last forever, on a heart and soul level.

Spiritual Philosophy

I believe we are all equal. I believe in God. I believe that God loves everybody the same. I believe in miracles. I believe that everybody is sent to this earth with something to give and to share and the ultimate thing that God wants us to do is love each other. I think that the most important thing isn't money, education, possessions, or power. It's about loving each other and taking care of each other and caring for each other. The same time you're giving you're getting back. It's a continual exchange. When I got sick with cancer six years ago, I had so many people on the street praying for me and making me cards. These guys that live in a camp and don't have any money went and got a card and sent it to me.

I love Tony Robbins' philosophy that you can change anything at any time. I believe anything is possible. So I've said to people, "I'm gonna believe in you until you believe in yourself again."

Advice for Others on Service

Service is giving of yourself, your time, your money, your belongings, your beliefs, your talents, your gifts, your love. You can be of service by volunteering your time in the kitchen. You can be of service by donating money to the Breast Cancer Foundation. You can be of service to your neighbors who don't have food or to a child that needs some help or to someone in your family. It's about stopping, with everything else that's going on in the world, and looking around and seeing where somebody needs some help or some support, and then maybe just listening, just doing whatever is needed to be of service.

It's a gift you give to yourself, and why not? Why not, when there's so much abundance in the world, why not look around and see how you can help and make a difference? Being able to help someone is really fulfilling. People should look at what gifts they have and share them. If you can sing, offer an educational workshop, volunteer with the kids, or donate sleeping bags, anything you do to help can make a difference; it's all important. Share your gifts.

Personal Perspective on COTS

COTS is hope. COTS is goodness. COTS staff are caring, diverse people. Everybody brings something to the table. We're sort of like a tree. COTS is the base and the tree has all these different programs and all these different people that add and bring things to it.

COTS is the best job I've ever had. It's not really a job. It's like God said, *"Michelle, while you are on this earth, I want you to be doing this."* So a lot of times I feel blissful about what I get to do.

I really love my life. I'm very thankful for it, and for my 13 years at COTS.

I left COTS and went back to real estate, after thirteen years. It was time for me to go, but I still have the connections that I made during those years. Those connections are still there in a million different ways, and I cherish them. I cherish the relationships, I cherish the people.

I still help people; they still call me for help, to go to detox or whatever they need, and now they're calling me when they want to buy a house too! I sold houses to three people who used to be homeless that I worked with before. It's like coming full circle.

You Came To Me Crying

By Michelle Baynes

trying to hide your tears
telling me that yesterday you had taken the Greyhound to San Francisco

you stood on the Golden Gate Bridge for an hour and a half
you didn't jump

today
you are here
asking for help

telling me that you have only been homeless
three days
last night you were sleeping by the Petaluma river

someone threatened to kill you
you ran staying up all night
afraid to sleep

you tell me that
you haven't eaten for three days
tomorrow you will buy a bus ticket and

"Go away"

you used to give seminars
$800.00 a hit
lost your house to foreclosure

I need to find a thread of hope
to believe that you won't kill yourself

I tell you that one day your life will be better than it ever was
that these are the times you will learn some of the most important things in life

that I don't think you're crazy
that there is hope
that you have a wife and two children

today you're clean and sober
today you got a job
tonight you have to sleep on the street

I leave

driving home

thinking

I must believe

Pat Grinnell

"Life is so fragile
and it can change in an instant."

Background

Pat Grinnell grew up in Napa, California and in Lagunitas, California, the second of four children. Her dad was in sales, but he was also a "renaissance man" who could repair things, cook fine dishes, and create works of art. Pat's mom worked as a clerk in a small Lagunitas grocery store. In Lagunitas, located in Marin County's San Geronimo valley, Pat's family lived in "a beautiful redwood house in the trees." Yet, despite his many talents, Pat's father was not a reliable parent; he was alcoholic, abusive, and unfaithful to his wife, and he often abandoned the family, only to return home and begin the cycle all over again. Pat recalls that even though her family dwelled in a gorgeous home, there were times when they scarcely had money for food, and one time they actually had to cut up and burn furniture in order to heat the house. Pat moved to Petaluma with her boyfriend (now her husband) after graduating from high school in 1978. She went on to get her Nurse Practitioner license at UC Davis, and has been volunteering at COTS since 1994, performing TB screening and other health services, as well as offering health education, for COTS clients.

Taking Care

I think I was destined to be a caretaker, because my parents were so irresponsible. I felt responsible for taking care of the house and my siblings when I was very young. One time my mom had said that she was going to kill herself, and we were in the process of moving to a different house. My dad came in and reported in a lackadaisical way that my mom had said that she was going to kill herself. I remember getting on my bike, because our old house was about ten blocks away, thinking that maybe she was over there. It was midnight, but I got on my bike, because I was determined to save her.

My parents' relationship was odd in that they had never gotten divorced. Sometimes my dad was with her and sometimes not. I was the one who took care of my mom after she got diagnosed with lung cancer at the age of 52. She died eight months later. I was giving her a bath in bed, and I called my brother to help me turn her. We'd just turned her over on her side and were putting on some of her favorite powder, and she took her last breath. It was the most profound event of my life.

I realized, in an instant, how quickly life can be over. I had asked my mom while she was sick, "Mom, if you had anything to do differently, what would you have done?" And she shared many things. She definitely would have divorced my dad, and she said she would have taken much better care of her teeth. And I wanted to *make a difference*. Life is so short. I think we are here to connect and be of service to other people.

Growing Up

I was raised Catholic, and attended mass regularly. That was probably the only stable thing in my life then. I never knew if my parents would get along, or whether or not they'd be drinking or using drugs. Church and prayers were very meditative for me. The Church taught a lot about loving one another and practicing the Golden rule, basic stuff but so important.

The funny thing about our house in Lagunitas is that years later, it became an ashram! To me that just fits perfectly. A place full of so much pain and misery in my life became a place of prayer and meditation.

I was always working. When I was twelve, I baby-sat. I wanted and needed to get out of my house, so I was always very motivated to work. I also cleaned houses, and then when I was sixteen I got a job as a hostess and food server at a retirement center in Marin. Then my husband and I moved up here to Petaluma. I had an aunt that was in nursing. I was seventeen, and I wanted to try something different, so I became a nurse's aide at a nursing home in Petaluma. I liked (and still like) working with older people, mainly because of their stories and the wisdom they share.

I went to nursing school at Santa Rosa Junior College for my licensed vocational nurse degree, so I was working and in school. I had just gotten married. Then, about the time I got pregnant with Daniel, my older son, I decided I wanted to become a Registered Nurse, so I went back to school for that. When my mom died, I went back to school for my Nurse Practitioner license. As I said, my mom's death was a profound experience; it gave me a new outlook.

I feel healed from my childhood. And these days, being in nature—hiking, running, breathing—is my spiritual practice.

Hooking Up with COTS

What brought me into contact with COTS was Genevieve Dean, an RN coworker and friend. She happened to mention in passing that she did work at the homeless shelter, and I was intrigued, probably because there had been so many times that my family had been close to being homeless—we were on welfare—and I felt that I needed to see what that was all about. Gen said, "Come on down sometime, and I'll show you around," and that's how it began, in 1994.

What I started out doing—and still do—is meet with residents, do TB screening and testing for them, obtain their health histories, and just connect with them. I also try to provide health education.

One time, the day before Thanksgiving, I was at the shelter and I noted the families working together, cooperating, putting together a Thanksgiving meal, and sitting at the table. I thought, "I wish I could have had a family like *this*--!" They were a community sharing together, having so little and giving so much. It just touched me very, very deeply.

I remember a teenage resident at COTS, who had the look of a juvenile delinquent: chains, piercings and all. This kid seemed pretty tough and we didn't talk too much while I gave him the TB skin test. Then he came back in and brought this black locked-up toolbox with him. And I thought, *Oh great, what's he gonna show me—a drug stash? Burglary tools?* But then—and I literally get chills thinking about this—he unlocked the box, and inside was a full collection of *Goosebumps* books.

At COTS, people are honest and open, and real. I admire that. You never know what's going to present itself when you go there. What happened to the person who was in a crisis last week? Who am I going to meet over there tonight? What will they have to share? I think of the families there that connect with and support one another, and even the ones that don't. I remember an African American gal who was a hardcore substance abuser, and she looked pretty hopeless. But after two or three weeks at COTS, she cleaned up her act! She had a bunch of kids, and I could identify with her son—it looked like he was responsible for taking care of everybody. But she really got it together! It was amazing!

A lot of times, people just need someone to listen to them, not to tell them what they need to do. Just listen to where they're coming from right then and there. And that's what I try to do.

Challenges

Some of the women and kids have suffered abuses, and that's really challenging. I get attached to some of the families that come, and am really hopeful for them to succeed, and sometimes that doesn't pan out.

But I remember when I was nursing in the hospital, one of the counselors in the recovery unit said, "You just never know when that one little intervention, that one kind word, that one little thing that you do, can help even a down-in-the-gutter drunk turn their life around." So I've always got that little glimmer of hope—there could be that one tiny little intervention, one kind word, one small thing, that makes a huge difference.

I feel like I grow too, because I see parts of myself in the stories residents share and the struggles they go through. People stereotype the homeless. I want to educate people to realize that no, they are you or me, and it could happen to anyone.

What It's All About

My sons have been at the shelter doing some of the work, too. I remember one time, my older son came home and said, "Mom, I think I'm going to put some of my stuff together and bring it down to COTS and just give it to the kids." They used to hate me leaving—"But Mom, you need to help me with homework." or "Can't you just stay home tonight?" Once I had them come down to the shelter, they saw what it was all about.

It has been a real eye-opener to just see how little we really need to get by. I have a friend who has this huge home, and I think, "Wow, five bedrooms, all these bathrooms—probably about fifteen families could live here." COTS has colored the way I see things. It has shaped my thoughts, and my life.

My family has downsized, we're living in a smaller home, trying to minimize possessions, living more simply, and feeling truly thankful for our health and other blessings. COTS has made me acutely aware and appreciative of all my blessings.

My husband works with inmates at San Quentin. So his big concern when I first started working at COTS was safety. Are there any ex-cons at the shelter? But now he says, "Wow, I'm so glad you do this for the community, that you make a difference that way," and he's felt inspired to give something back to the community too, volunteering with the Wilmar Fire Department.

Philosophy

I think it comes down to the Golden Rule: treat others the way you want to be treated. You think that your life sucks, that everything is so bad, but then you get into a group, or you're talking to friends, and you realize that everybody is struggling, everybody has problems, and yours are probably not so bad compared to the ones some people have. See how their experiences have made them who they are, just like your experiences are shaping you.

Service and Facing Fears

Service is about doing something to improve the quality of life for others, without expecting something in return. COTS has been my cause celebre. I think that, whatever you fear, whether it's homeless people, the mentally ill, drug addicts—whatever you fear, I think those are the places that you need to go.

If you get involved with whomever it is that you fear, it opens you up and you realize that your fear is really based on nothing.

I trust my intuition. If I feel that something isn't safe, I know how to keep a boundary. With time, you get a better sense of how and when to do that.

Life is so frail, and it can change in an instant. When I was eleven years old, I was down in Los Angeles, staying with my grandparents one summer. I was walking near Occidental College with my aunt and her friend. We had just swum at the college and were walking home. We looked behind and there was a gang of kids chasing after us. I was able to run fast and get away, but my aunt and her friends were beaten awfully, earrings ripped out and everything, by these gang members. And I remember looking over at a man who was on one of those ride-on mowers. He saw this going on, and he just kept mowing his lawn. I remember thinking, why didn't he get involved to stop this violence? But he didn't, and there were other adults around too that didn't.

So it's a basic choice you have to make: you get involved, or you don't.

Mike Hatfield

"If you didn't ever think about yourself, you wouldn't eat. You wouldn't last very long. But life is more than that."

Background

Mike Hatfield has worked in telecommunications since he left college in 1984. He is a long-time financial supporter and advisor to COTS.

Family Background

My mother is from Ohio and my father is from Missouri. But I grew up and attended college in Indiana. I have one sister who is a couple of years younger.

My mother volunteered often. She was involved in a program with seniors where they would go and visit. It was like Big Brother/Big Sister reversed. Each volunteer sort of inherited an older person and went and spent time with them, perhaps once or twice a month. They would just go and sit and have tea with them or whatever.

My mom was also a driver for Meals on Wheels for quite a while when I was a kid. I would be with her in the car when she was doing Meals on Wheels. I don't recall helping her with it, but I was definitely there with her. These are the kinds of things parents give to kids that they take with them the rest of their lives.

I think that seeing what my mother did influenced my attitude about service.

Volunteering

My first experience volunteering was in college. My fraternity would host Christmas parties for underprivileged children in the area; we'd bring them in and give them a Christmas party and Christmas presents.

We also were responsible for hosting, in Indiana, the Area 7 Special Olympics, a regional Special Olympics. It's a big thing. There are probably 400 athletes who participate. Our fraternity was responsible for that and I actually ran it one year.

You get a sense of how much work it takes to do something. You can imagine all the Special Olympics events that happen across the country and this is just one small thing. You realize how much effort is involved and the fact that it is all done by volunteers. That's the first time I got a perspective of what it takes. Before that I thought these things just happened; the government must pay for these things and they just happen.

Then I was a Literacy Reader, or teacher, helping adults learn to read.

COTS and Homelessness

One thing that impacted me was the realization that people find themselves homeless for purely economic reasons. I used to share the popular perception that homelessness only happens to drug addicts or mentally ill people or people who aren't functional on some level. But actually there were a number of people who, by every measure, are functioning well, but yet still not able to make it.

It is an artifact of our economy that there are some people who are less advantaged than others. At what point do we move outside of the market forces and try to influence that? There's a challenge--how can you shift everyone forward? There is an unequal distribution of income but what can we do to help the people who are at the bottom of the ladder improve continuously and make their lot in life better by continuing to improve?

COTS is an organization that is really doing something and making a difference, and that's something I'm attracted to. There are a lot of people who want to do good and talk about it but it's hard to see what the results are. It's pretty obvious what the results are at COTS and it's easy to get behind that.

Service

Service is an aspect of community and stems from the fact that we're all connected and interrelated.

Everyone is going to have their own self-interest. That's fundamental to human nature. If you didn't ever think about yourself you wouldn't eat. You wouldn't last very long. But life is more than that.

As an individual in a community, whatever size, whether a city or state, you benefit from being a part of it. You don't have to work to benefit from it. It just happens. When you're a part of community you just get simple things like roads, stop signs, and various services and support. You'd have to work really, really, really hard to not benefit from what's there. You're not just out there on your own.

Since you benefit from community in some way, it seems to me you've got to give back to it. If everybody's just taking, it can't work. It's like an energy source. If you're constantly taking from the batteries and never charging them, they are going to be drained.

You should look around and say, "I'm benefiting from this and therefore I should contribute back." There's lots of opportunity to do it. There's not one right form to do it.

Find something that interests you or where you have something to offer and start with that. Get started doing it and then when you do it, it will become even more clear why it makes sense to continue to do it.

Service isn't that hard, it doesn't take that much time, and you get satisfaction out of it. It's the starting of it that people just don't know to do.

Learning service is like learning to do anything. If you've never done it before, someone's got to help you take that first step. It's the same as if you're going to go play golf for the first time or go skiing for the first time. It's helpful having someone say, "Hey, let's go skiing. It's not so bad." Or "Let's go try this." Once you try it you say, "Oh, okay. I get this."

I think for me there was certainly a seed that got planted when I was growing up and saw what my mother did. But actually participating and seeing and understanding and knowing that my volunteering directly benefited somebody--that was the real catalyst for me to get much more involved.

I think it's a pretty simple thing. It's having the capacity to help and seeing the obvious need and then saying, "Why shouldn't I?" It's the right thing to do. It's not much more complicated than that.

Not everyone who gets involved in service is going to say, "Oh, my life has changed." But when even a small group of people get together, in a relatively small amount of time they can make a big impact.

Mike Johnson

*"Everybody is human and no matter
how wretched they are, they need human
contact and respect."*

Background

*As Mike Johnson was growing up, his family of four moved from San Francisco,
California, to Berkeley, California, to New York, back to Berkeley, and back to San
Francisco. In San Francisco, Mike's father left the family and his mother remarried
shortly thereafter. When Mike entered middle school, he left his mother, stepfather, and
sister, and went to Terra Linda, California to live with his uncle. Immediately out of high
school Mike moved into an apartment with his girlfriend; they married but had a strife-
ridden relationship that broke up several times before they finally divorced when Mike was
23. Having had alcohol abuse modeled to him as a child, Mike developed a drinking
habit to ease his pain, which eventually landed him on the streets. Mike was homeless for
eight years, before getting clean and sober in 1999 and being hired by COTS, where he
now serves as Assistant Executive Director and Director of Programs. In 2003, Mike
married Tracy Lenzi, who was then a COTS case manager.*

Childhood

Up until the time I was ten or eleven, while my father was still living
with us, we did fairly well. We traveled a lot and my father made good
money. But then he left us in San Francisco, in the middle of the Mission

district. My mother had some secretarial skills, but she wasn't able to support the family the way that we had been used to. So we were in pretty dire straits. I spent a lot of time on the streets, shining shoes and hustling to clothe myself and get by, because my mom just couldn't do it all. From an early age I was no stranger to poverty and what poverty can do to people and to families.

All the kids that I grew up with at that time in San Francisco were poor. Most of the fathers were deadbeat dads, and the moms were on welfare. The kids were unsupervised and unruly and hustling the streets to survive. The older ones were on their way to prison or worse. That was the backdrop of my life at that point. It was pretty seedy, but I didn't really notice it that much. When you're a kid, your outlook is a little bit different. You take a lot of things for granted. Your situation is the way it is; you don't really compare it to anything. You just deal with it as it goes. There were a lot of things that I liked about that way of life; there was a lot of freedom. I came and went as I wanted; I didn't have a whole lot of supervision. I came home from school and I'd have the run of the house and the neighborhood until my mom got home. And even then, she was too tired to do much. So I spent a lot of time watching the workings of a poor neighborhood, and that imprinted on me the destruction that can happen when people aren't fed right and are making bad choices. Most of the older brothers and sisters of the kids I was hanging out with were selling dope to survive. I saw prostitution and gangs, and though I didn't really understand at the time what was going on, those things made quite an impression on me.

Leaving Home

Then my mother took up with this guy who was a musician. He was on SSI because of emotional disabilities; he was a drug user and alcoholic, and he and my mom had a whirlwind relationship; it took them two weeks to decide that they wanted to get married. She was all for it, because she really needed somebody in her life, and she picked this man because he was the exact opposite of my father. He was a no-account—romantic, idealistic, and screwed up—whereas my father had been so focused on his career that he had nothing left for the family. But this new man drove a wedge between me and my mother. He wasn't my father, but he was trying to be and I just couldn't accept it, so I fought his authority tooth and nail from day one. He couldn't take it, and after a couple years of constantly battling with me, my mother and he decided that living with me just wasn't working, so I got sent to live with my uncle in Terra Linda.

I don't think any kid benefits from being shuffled around by family members. In the long run, it was a good decision to relocate me into a different environment, but the rejection, the feelings of not being wanted, were devastating to me. It was like, "Wow, this is sort of the last straw: my father leaves, and now my mother—my *mother*—is choosing this monster over her own son." So that was a huge blow, but I couldn't have done any better if I'd stayed in that situation. My self-esteem would have been under attack on a daily basis if I had. At least the way that it happened, I was able to move on. My sister, on the other hand, didn't have that opportunity, and she paid dearly for it, later in life. Her self-esteem and sense of self-worth were very damaged for many years after my mother and my stepfather finally did break up. But she's doing great now; she owns her own house, she makes great money, she's happily married.

Living in Marin County

So moving to Marin County was probably the best thing that had ever happened to me up to that point, because it took me out of a really bad situation, just as I was starting middle school. It was definitely a culture shock, moving from the poorest section of the Mission district in San Francisco to the most affluent community in California. The parents of my new friends all had houses and cars and their kids had all the things that they wanted, but I was still poor. My uncle was a property manager, and had just started managing a subsidized housing complex in Marin, so his salary was very low, but he had a pretty apartment. He was a taskmaster, and I spent a lot of time after school cleaning up the apartments to earn my keep, raking lawns and sweeping and pruning and mowing. At the time, it didn't seem fair; my friends had jobs for earning money while I was earning my dinner.

By the time I got to high school, I felt a little bit more at home. But still, I had come from a much different background than most of the kids. In high school, I didn't have my own car, like most of my friends did, and I didn't live in a house; I lived in an apartment. I wasn't able to try out for sports because I was working for my uncle after school. But I learned how to work, and that work ethic served me well in the years to come. I fought it at the time; I had fantasies of breaking my ankle or my arm on purpose just to get out of doing all this stuff. Luckily I never followed through with those fantasies.

Marriage and Work

Midway through my junior year, I met a girl from a different school. We fell in love and moved in together after I graduated. We eventually got married. We ended up moving into my uncle's apartment complex; he worked it so that we could get in at the top of the list for Section 8 housing, under her name. But it was a very rocky relationship. It ended five years later, after many breakups.

The first couple of years we lived together, I went to community college, studying architecture and the history of art and drafting and English lit and a few other subjects, trying to find something I could do. I wanted to do something in the technical arts, but after talking with my father, I was discouraged from the field of architecture, which was his, because I didn't have the math skills to see me through school. My math skills were extremely deficient. My grades in other classes were pretty good, but not enough to get me into a decent state school, so I gave up on that dream. I did a lot of drawing and illustration and renderings for buildings, but never attempted to make a profession out of it. I'm sorry I didn't now; I think I probably could have handled the math if I had sought some help or tutoring.

Also, I was working: selling everything from clothing to clocks. For a kid just coming out of high school in Marin county, there was very little else to do besides work in retail. But shortly before my wife and I broke up for good, I started working the trades. A friend of my uncle's needed help doing some remodeling on his house. I was between jobs, so I started working with him, and discovered that I had some ability with my hands. I worked with this guy and started to get a feel for carpentry and drywall and that sort of thing. My father was a general contractor at the time and he was doing a lot of building work back east so I ended up going to Manhattan to work for my dad for a summer.

That was a good experience. My dad had had a real hard time relating to his kids before they were old enough to carry a conversation. He didn't have the patience to be a father. But when you're in your formative years you're willing to forgive all of that, I think, just because you need your dad so much. Regardless of what other male role models you have, your natural father is always the one that you're going to be gravitating towards for guidance. Despite how he had conducted himself as a father, I respected him—his opinion, his insight, anything he had to say. Whereas with other people in my life, like my stepfather and my uncle, very little of what they said made much of an impression.

So what my dad had to say was important to me. And he told me at that point, when I was working back east, that the thing for a young man to do is work the trades—you can make good money at it; you don't need to go to school; you can learn everything you need to know on the job. So that's what I did. I did carpentry and drywall and anything I could get my hands on. My wife and I had gone to LA to be with her family for a little while, and she ended up taking off and coming back up here. But I stayed, and got into doing set-building work, which was extremely interesting—a whole different way of doing things. It was all very superficial in its construction, but the methods and the techniques that they used were fascinating, very fast paced, never a dull moment. After I had my fill of that I came back up to Sonoma County. At the time my father was doing a huge development project with a partner of his in San Francisco, and they needed help on that, so I signed onto his crew to help build these things. That gave me tile setting experience, which was my last involvement in trades before I became homeless.

Alcoholism and Descent Into Homelessness

In Los Angeles, after my wife and I broke up, I had started drinking. It had gotten steadily worse, though I was able to function. I was disposed to drink from my early childhood, because both my mom and my father were functioning alcoholics. Their idea of drinking was "never before 5," but my drinking was different; it was a response to my pain, an attempt to blot out my feelings of inadequacy and poor self esteem. I drank enough during the day so that I didn't have to feel that depth of hurt. But alcoholism is a progressive disease, and soon I was drinking more and more to maintain the same buzz. It took a while, but my health started to deteriorate, my energy level fell, my concentration was poor. I started making mistakes, and employers began to notice that I was nipping a little bit during the day.

I moved into my mom's house. Just the fact that I was moving in with my mom was another nail in the coffin of my self esteem, so things got even worse. I was drinking mornings and throughout the day, even while I was working. I didn't drink to the point where I had blackouts or staggered or slurred, but I would drink just about up to that point every day, so I had a lot of trouble getting work, and I pretty much burned all my bridges. IF I showed up to work, I did good work. IF I made it back from my lunch break on time, I did good work. But often I just didn't show up and didn't call. I never got any complaints on the actual work that I did, but the drinking affected everything else, and my life fell apart. My mom was sick of seeing me destroying myself. I was gaining weight, I had a pasty complexion, I would come home from work and fall right asleep.

I couldn't control the drinking; it was probably up to a quart a day. And I neglected all the little things you have to do to keep your life in order, like registering your vehicle, keeping your license valid, paying your rent, telephone bills, those sort of things. One by one, things just fell apart. My phone bill was huge, I was months behind in my rent, my truck was unregistered for six months. My license was suspended, and I was still driving the truck every day, until I got pulled over and it got taken away. And that incident was what finally tipped the scales. My mother couldn't stand the idea of me being stuck in her house all day long, without any way to support myself or contribute to the rent. She threw me out in November of 1991.

I had a friend that lived in Petaluma, and he came and picked me up—me, my sleeping bag and my suitcase—and dropped me off in Walnut Park. He was also living with his mother and had no place to put me up.

Life on the Streets, and First Contacts with COTS

I had always had some place to live, even if it wasn't all that great. I'd had a roof over my head; there was always some sort of safety net in my life. But now, I found myself totally alone, alienated from my entire family.

I began sleeping at the side of the river down on First Street, down by the grain storage places. I spent five days wandering around the park area until it was time to sleep, and I had no food, just water. Five days. On my fifth day of sitting on the bench in Walnut Park, this guy—Mike something or other, I can't remember his last name—had been watching me do this dance around the park all this time, day after day. He said to me, "You know, you look a little bit hungry."

By this time I must have looked like I was starving, because I was. Five days without food and without alcohol, too, I might add. I was suicidal. If there had been a way I could have killed myself at that point, I would have. If I'd had a gun, or some sort of fast-acting poison, I would have used it. I remember laying there on my sleeping bag, trying to think up ways that wouldn't be too painful. I couldn't come up with anything—I had no rope, there was no razor blade.

But on the fifth day, when I was at the end of my rope, this guy told me, "You know, if you walk down D Street, there's a soup kitchen down there. It's only about half a mile down the road. If you're hungry, why don't you go on there and eat?" I said, "Are you kidding? There's a place I can get something to eat?"

I hustled down D Street, I walked in the door of the kitchen. I nearly collapsed out of sheer gratitude. I don't think I was ever so happy to walk into any door of any building in my life. After that meal, I thought, "Maybe I can survive now." Here I was destitute, starving, and there was a room full of people in the same situation that I was in, but they were all laughing and talking and there was a sense of community. I thought, "Well, if they can do it, if they're surviving, hell, I can do it, too." So that was a pivotal. I learned that with a little bit of help you can get past anything—you can come back from the brink. So I spent many years dependent on that kitchen, and then, later on, the Opportunity Center.

I and others like me on the street at the time were sleeping in the Armory at night during winter, cleaning ourselves in the Walnut Park bathrooms and various service station rest rooms, and getting fed at the Kitchen. But we had no place to get really cleaned up or get access to any other services. I was homeless from 1991 until 1999.

My original contact with COTS came just after the Armory closed and I started frequenting the Opportunity Center. Michelle Baynes would come around to the parks, letting people know that the Op Center was going to be opening at a certain time. At that time, there were no facilities in Petaluma that offered showers, laundry, telephones, or any of the basic services that we provide now. So, initially, for four or five years, I used the Opportunity Center just to take care of basic needs, and the rest of my time I spent servicing my addictions, alcoholism and, later on, methamphetamines. I didn't really have a lot of time for counseling and that sort of thing; I was too busy running the streets.

I stole to support my drinking; I committed petty theft and other crimes. Hard-core alcoholism will make you do just about anything. My crimes got worse, from misdemeanors to felonies, and the jail sentences got longer. But I continued to drink until I got liver jaundice and a doctor told me that I had about a year or so of time left if I continued at my rate of consumption. I think I spent another six months drinking after that, before I finally quit.

Speed

I think what facilitated my quitting alcohol was taking up another drug, speed. Once I got a taste of that I forgot all about the alcohol. I didn't know anything about AA or NA or the concepts and principles of addiction; I didn't realize that substituting one for another was the same disease; I thought I was doing the right thing. I congratulated myself for having put alcohol aside in favor of a different drug that I only used sporadically. I had no income to support a day-to-day speed habit, so it was something I did when I could get it, and the rest of the time I was straight—relatively straight, anyway. So I felt pretty good about myself at that point; I felt, "Well, you've put away the really bad stuff. And hell, this is all very new and exciting. There's a whole different crowd of people; methamphetamine users have a whole different lifestyle from drunks. Their craziness has a much more interesting edge." The drug facilitates that—you get the hallucinations, the sleep deprivation, you get all these different interesting by-products of using, whereas with alcohol, you just drink and fade.

So it felt fine at first, but it took its toll. Even though I wasn't using it that frequently, speed would keep me up for days at a time, and then when I came down, I might eat if I could, but sometimes I couldn't even make it to the kitchen; I just had to stay where I was until I detoxified. When I did speed, I never stole to support my habit. I couldn't do it—I just didn't have the nerve to be a burglar. There wasn't any way that I was going to hold up or strong-arm somebody; it just wasn't in me. But there were other ways of supporting a habit, if it's very small. If all you need is twenty dollars to get yourself a fix, you can find things at the Goodwill and sell them, or you can trade things for dope. There's always something going on—collecting cans on a good night, that sort of thing. Being a broker for other people was probably the easiest way to do it; once you found connections that were fairly reliable, then there'd always be somebody that wanted something. You'd facilitate the sale and get a piece of it. It was a very insidious, sick lifestyle.

Pivotal Events

Now I was still coming around to the Op Center, and Michelle had been pushing me for a couple of years to get back in contact with my folks, so I finally did. That was when I learned that my grandfather on my father's side had died, and had left me almost ten thousand dollars. I made all kinds of plans: "Ten thousand dollars—wow!" After spending eight, nine years on the street with nothing, that was a huge windfall! So I thought, "Well, this is my ticket out. This is my chance to get out of this situation, get some transportation, a place to live, and I can find work." Forgetting all the while that I was a speed addict!

So when I got the money I moved into a local motel and the party started. It took about three weeks, and then the money was gone.

I bought a van that I couldn't drive because I wasn't careful about who I bought it from, and the guy that sold it to me had switched the plates from a vehicle that he had totaled. I found out this when I got pulled over by the Rohnert Park police. So that was twenty-three hundred dollars down the tubes right there, and the rest of it was blown on motels and speed. It had been an ongoing twenty-four hour marathon until it was completely exhausted. At the tail end of that process I was leaving one motel room to go pick up a backpack that I'd left at another motel that I had just exited from. And some other people that I knew were in that room, and they had my backpack there. It was midnight and I decided for some odd reason that I had to have this backpack. I got the thing out of the room and I'm just walking out the door and this police officer that had arrested me several times in the past for paraphernalia and so forth, who knew my drug history, saw me come walking out of this motel room that wasn't rented to me, and he pulls me over and checks me out, and I'm obviously intoxicated. He searches me to find if I have something on me; I'm under the influence— that's three months mandatory, right there. It's my third possession conviction, so that's a felony, too.

That woke me up. I thought, "Oh my God, I've got a felony. I'm looking at twelve months at least." Up until this point the longest jail sentence

I'd done was 120 days, and that was, to me, the longest four months of my life. I didn't think I could do twelve months. I just didn't think I could handle it without going absolutely crazy. As it turned out, because it was my first felony, I was able to get supervised probation. So that took care of the felony, but I still had to do time for driving under the influence. Still, after I found out that I wasn't going to be doing a year, it gave me some optimism. I decided I was done with the lifestyle—I had just spent ten thousand dollars of my grandfather's money for nothing; I had absolutely nothing to show for it, and was in worse shape physically, emotionally, spiritually, financially, than I was before I got it. So I knew at that point just how screwed up I was from doing the drugs. Once I figured that out, I knew that it had to stop. That was a fork in the road of my life—the realization that I had no control when it came to the speed.

Before I came to that crossroad, I had had a pattern for years: I'd use speed for a couple of days, and then recover from that until the next time that I was able to do it. When I had drugs, I would get out on the streets and use, and then, when I started to get hungry and tired of being dirty, I would come in and use COTS' services and just hang out and recuperate until the next time came around. That pattern repeated itself innumerable times over the years. There were attempts made by the COTS staff to intervene, but it wasn't a forceful intervention; it was sort of a gentle prodding. The program that we have in place now wouldn't allow for that sort of behavior. I would have been called on it much sooner. That may be a good thing, but it's quite possible that I never would have made the connection that I made later on if I had been denied service on the basis of my addiction during those years. I don't think any coercion would have worked. I would have ended up bitter. On the other hand, because I was so dependent on COTS at the time—for meals, for clothes, for everything, really—having my services denied might have jump-started my decision-making process. There's really no way of knowing at this point. It's a hard call, and a difficult balance for COTS.

At any rate, in the end, when I was ready, COTS was there. Michelle was there; the other staff were there; they knew that I was really ready.

Working for COTS

So in jail, for the two months that I was there, it took me away from drugs long enough for me to get some clarity and get my mind back together. Before going in, I asked Michelle if there was a possibility I could get hired when I got out, because I knew that I needed to work, I needed something to hold on to, something to reach for. Without it, I was afraid that I would relapse and go back to the same old lifestyle and wind up in prison. And I hated the idea of being locked up! I talked to Brad Silvestro too, and I said, "Brad, look, I'm really ready to make some changes. I know that I need to work when I get out, or else I don't think I'll be able to make it, I don't think I'll be able to stop myself from going back into this." And Brad said, "Yeah, we'll put you to work when you get out."

That really took faith on their part! Just the year before, I had been given a chance to work at the winter shelter, which didn't work out too well. I was hired even though I was still using. I think Michelle had been hoping that I would come out of it at least long enough to do my job there, but it didn't work out that way. As soon as I started getting paychecks, I was using again. Having an income, for an addict, is not a good thing. It just gave me more money to spend on drugs. So I ended up getting let go. But that experience gave me a taste of working again, which was a good thing.

When I got out of jail for the last time in October of 1999, I was ready to commit to my recovery. I'd spent a lot of years using COTS—using the services, being a drain on resources, not really doing anything for myself or for anybody else. I knew in my heart that it was only right to give something back. They hired me as a site monitor at the Opportunity Center. If I hadn't been employed at COTS, I think I probably would have tried to volunteer in some way. There were other things I believe I could have done for work— the types of things that I did in the past, construction or trade work and so forth. That might have paid more, or been more comfortable because it was something that I knew. But COTS just felt right, though I was worried at first that the atmosphere—seeing the old people, watching them doing all the same things that I used to do—would be a problem. But it never was.

I worked my way up through the ranks at COTS. I started with part-time work, moving up to the site supervisor for the Kitchen, then Director of the Mary Isaak Center, and recently was promoted to Assistant Executive Director and Director of Programs. My work at COTS satisfies my need to be involved with other people, and to help them make the changes that I did. Once you see people change, it's difficult to get satisfaction like that from anything else; it's sort of a fix in its own way. All the time that I spent working in the trades and doing different construction projects, that had its own satisfactions—the satisfaction of having done a job well, and having made your clients happy. But watching somebody stop hurting themselves and start helping themselves—that's just a great feeling; it's something that you can't get in any other line of work.

There's a lot of people that we're serving now that I've known for years, and it's really a kick when you see somebody that you've known out on the streets and used with and so forth, make some good choices for themselves. You feel like a cheerleader.

The Homeless Are Human

It's difficult to know when someone's asking for another chance and they're sincere. The population that we serve has a lot of very wily people. When people are on the streets, their survival mode sharpens their ability to manipulate people and systems to get what they need. So you just have to take them at their word and hope for the best. You have to wonder, if they spent that much energy and put that much thought into doing something constructive, how successful they would be! It's always a good thing when you find out later on that they really were telling you the truth. It's just so refreshing when that happens.

Everybody is human, and no matter how wretched they are, they need human contact and respect. Above all, they need dignity. I lived with people on the street that, if you saw them walking down the street, you'd think, "Oh my god, I don't want to get close to that person; they're so filthy." But if you spend some time talking to them, you find out that they're a person under all that. So it angers me when I hear judgments being made about "The Homeless." It's very pervasive in our society—judging people on the basis of their appearance. I think people need to be judged on who they are, not what they look like or even what they're doing with their lives. As long as people aren't hurting themselves or each other, I don't think they should be judged or treated with less respect than anybody else would be treated.

I've had people look at me with disgust the same way that I see people looking at other homeless people with disgust. It's a sickening thing, really, having been there myself and having known a lot of people that have been there and are still in that position. People who are on the street aren't necessarily there by choice. They're victims of themselves, but they're also victims of the world that we live in. And a lot of them are not equipped to deal with all the obstacles that have been placed in front of them— sometimes, unwittingly, by themselves. Our society's very intolerant of homeless people. We'll send billions in dollars in aid to other countries to rebuild their infrastructure, their economies, and feed their people, and yet we have millions of people on the streets of America that are not being helped with the same respect and regard, and I think that's a horrible thing. I think charity begins at home, and we should do what we can for the people who are closest to us.

The Meaning of Service

Service means so many different things. Obviously, the first thing that comes to mind is helping other people, but there's a lot more to it than that, really. Somebody once told me that nobody ever does anything that's purely altruistic, and I've come to believe that that's really true. The times that you get the most out of life are always when you're giving the most. That's why Christmas is so popular. The act of giving yourself, especially when it doesn't involve an exchange of material items, is the most rewarding thing in life. So my idea of service is that process of being there when somebody needs you, and being able to offer them whatever you have to offer. Some of the most meaningful giving is sitting down and talking to another person.

Over the course of the years that I've spent with COTS, I've seen the most meaningful changes made in people's lives as a result of those sorts of interactions, be they with case managers or with each other.

When you dig into yourself, and you reveal experiences that you've had, or insights that you've gained, and you give those to another person, and it's given in a natural, friendly way where you're not expecting somebody else to reciprocate, then it's always received well. And if it's received well, then chances are it's going to make some impact on that person's life, maybe not right then, but you plant little seeds in people that way. It happens all the time in our daily lives, and you don't even realize that it's happening. And sometimes the effects of that give-and-take aren't felt for months or years down the road, but they happen. It happened to me. The connections that I had with Michelle—at the time that she and I were having those conversations, I didn't think it would amount to anything, but it did.

It's a positive energy flow. Things that you do that influence other people in a good way always feel better than things that you do that influence people in a bad way, regardless of what your material stake is. When you're on your deathbed and you're looking back on your life, those instances where you've been able to help other people and see in them that something positive has happened, *those* are the things that you'll remember. When you're ready to meet your maker, those are the kinds of things that stack up in your favor. I don't ever want to wind up, at the very end of my life, wondering what I'd done with it all, looking back and thinking, "My God, I wasted all that time chasing material stuff when I could have been spending more time with the family." I think it takes a while before people begin to break out of that kind of paper chase mentality. And I think being homeless for a length of time helps that! I think everybody should have that experience!

The Meaning of COTS

COTS' meaning to me has changed over the years. At first it was something to be taken for granted. I didn't spend a lot of time thinking about what COTS was about, what their mission was, what they were trying to do for me or for anybody, really. I was very much blinded to that.

But COTS is about helping people to help themselves, more than anything. It's about helping people to understand that they're worth the time and the effort to *be* helped.

COTS is about its people. You could have the most efficiently run agency in the world in the middle of your city, but if it's not staffed with people that care, that give a damn and understand what's going on, then it's not really gonna help, because it is those connections between the people that are involved that are really important and lasting, when it comes to influencing people's lives. And that's what we're in the business of doing. We're there to give of ourselves and our experiences and our wisdom when people are in a position to receive it, and where it might do them some good.

Volunteerism

Try it, you'll like it. Go into it with an open mind and heart. Put aside your judgments, your preconceptions, and just do it. If you want to understand the plight of others, you need to connect with them. The more people that understand the problems, the better the chances we're going to have, as a society, to solve those problems. You can have a few people that know exactly what's going on and how to fix our society's problems, but they're going to have a hard time if everyone else stays ignorant.

Brian Sobel

"Everyone has a role to play in helping to lift others."

Background

Brian Sobel was born in Tokyo, Japan, the son of an army officer. He spent most of his early years moving quite frequently, living in Europe and several parts of the United States. When Brian was a freshman in high school, his father was transferred to the Presidio in San Francisco. His family settled in San Rafael, California.

Brian attended San Francisco State University and majored in Broadcasting and Communications. He became a radio station news director for several years before taking a position in the Corporate Communications Department at Fireman's Fund Insurance. He moved to Petaluma in 1980.

Brian was soon involved in Petaluma politics, first serving on the Planning Commission, and then taking a temporary position on the City Council when councilmember Roland Bond passed away. He then ran for City Council in 1986 and 1990, and served two terms. He now runs his own political and communications consulting company, Sobel Communications.

Early Influences of Family

One thing that affected me profoundly is that I had a brother who was born with Down 's syndrome. I watched how hard my parents worked to give Matthew a life against some pretty long odds. I watched how they dealt with my brother's disability, and all the pressures that went with it, with such elegance. I learned a lot from that. And I watched the way people treated my brother, and that helped craft what kind of politician I wanted to be, what kind of office holder, what kind of person.

My mother was an Irish Catholic who followed people like Fulton J. Sheen and Padre Pio, and others. So very early on, she was always drumming into me the need to be charitable and to be fair.

But it was really from my father that I learned that it doesn't matter what a person's circumstances are; no one is any less a human being than anyone else. So, irrespective of rank and privilege, you should treat everybody the same.

Philosophy about the Government and Giving and Service

From the time I was a little boy, I always had a big interest in politics and I understood, very early on, that politicians can work two ways. You can be somebody who takes advantage, a "taker," or you can be a "giver." And I knew that if you combined politics and giving, and having a social conscience, that you could do a lot for people.

In my view, the government is here to help those that can't help themselves. That has been my guiding philosophy. Because of what I saw my brother go through, and a lot of people like my brother, and from moving all over the world and seeing people in different circumstances, I knew I had an opportunity even at the local level to really do some things to benefit others.

Role Models

My role models were plucked from different situations. I very much appreciate Hubert Humphrey. His attitudes and work ethic around seniors, around the disabled, absolutely mirrored mine. I read a lot about how Hubert Humphrey dealt with disability.

What I tried not to do is limit myself to people I felt an ideological connection with. I also wanted to approach other religions, other types of thinking. Of all the professors and teachers I ever had, the one who probably impacted me more than any other was a high school government teacher in San Rafael. She had been fired by a school district in Paradise, California because she was an avowed communist, and she ended up on the cover of *Life* magazine. She was the fairest and best teacher I ever had, though I would never subscribe to her philosophy of government. But what she taught me was "be open to everything, and then make up your own mind."

I was raised Roman Catholic and I was an altar boy. There were priests that I met along the way whom I found to be very genuine, beautiful human beings. I also met nuns, who were my instructors during the times I attended private school. Their service orientation was of benefit to me, the idea of giving something back, not caring so much about one's personal belongings and bank accounts and all that.

What I tried to do with that was to find a hybrid. I knew that if you went hat-in-hand all the time, you could do okay. But I was more of the mind to go hat-in-hand, but keep a club behind my back. I was willing to use either approach to get a program in place that I thought would help people. What I found in government was if you didn't pull that trigger too often, you were very powerful. The people who tried to pull the trigger all the time eventually exhausted everybody.

How Brian Became Involved with COTS

Laure Reichek and Mary Isaak came to me, now-Congresswoman Lynn Woolsey, and some other Council members and asked, "Do you think we could get a modest amount of money to do what needs to be done in this community?" I, along with others, said, "Sure, let's see if we can make something happen."

I'm proud that when I was a City Council member I voted for COTS when it was still just a concept. I was involved in the early years of COTS, helping COTS get funding from the city and other sources. I've always been a friend and staunch supporter.

All this money that we oversee ought to be taking care of real needs in the community.

If you take enough time to go out and actually speak with people who are homeless or who have had a rough turn in their lives, you find out they're every bit as educated as you are, their life stories are every bit as interesting as yours, and for the want of a break, they could be some other place and way ahead of you by societal standards.

I'll never forget one time I was in the Armory, and I saw a nice family. I remember sitting down and talking to the father. I said, "Would you care to tell me your circumstances?" And the fellow said, "I'm a roofer, by trade," and he said, "The roofing business is down." And then he stopped and he said, "By the way, can I ask you a question?" I said, "What's that?" And he said, "Do you have a family?" And I said, "Yes, I have a family." And he said, "So, if you were really down on your luck, would you have a brother or a sister or somebody you could call for 250 or 300 bucks?" and I said "Yes." And he said, "You want to know the difference between you and me?" And I said, "Please." And he said, "I don't have that call to make. My wife has no family, I have no family. I have nowhere to turn."

That was very profound because this is what throws people into these situations: they don't have the resources. COTS is a resource, but absent a COTS or something like that, they don't have family or options.

I never forgot that conversation and it very much guided the way I viewed my work as a member of the City Council and all of the regional boards. I held public office for a long time and I never forgot what that fellow told me. It's easy to draw assumptions about other people. You might think, "Well, there should be roofing work everywhere." But actually no, there wasn't roofing work everywhere. And when you get behind the eight-ball, you can get behind the eight-ball so quickly that you're struggling to maintain your life, forgetting about going and getting a job and waiting two weeks to get your first paycheck, and all those little things that we take for granted.

Brian's Connection with COTS

My role has had to do with cutting through governmental red tape and bureaucracy. You don't see my fingerprints on much, and that's by design. But I know a lot of people and it has been easy for me to pick up the phone and say, "By the by, this needs to happen." And a lot of it happens behind the scenes. I'll be at a dinner with somebody who doesn't quite believe in the mission, and by the end of the dinner, they believe in the mission! And because I have flown straight and not double crossed people, I can pick up the phone to Democrats and Republicans and Independents and Greens and everybody, and they know that I'm not going to lie to them. They know my intentions are genuine.

That's been my role. I've wanted to be there for COTS whenever COTS wanted me to be there, because I believe it is a meritorious organization doing great work. There's a huge amount of return on money that's spent helping people move on and have productive lives. If you look at it in purely business terms, just putting somebody back on the tax roll and making them productive is very beneficial to society. If people are self-sustaining and can get along without our services, those services can be given to somebody else. So through the years, I've always viewed the COTS program as a really well-run business.

Philosophy on Making a Difference

My core philosophy extends beyond COTS, and it goes back to that philosophy I cited earlier about what government is here for. I might even say it's what we're all here for: to help people who don't have the same advantages that we do.

It can be putting money in the church plate, it can be helping to serve a meal, it can be leaving an appropriate tip. It can be minor things that you do, but I think as we go through our day we have to think—and I fail all the time at this, but I try to remember to think—"Is there some way I can give something back?" It can be small. Sometimes starting with something small is how people first give it a try, and starting small usually leads to more and more, once people realize how it makes them feel, to give back. I think every human being ought to find an area where they can give back. I really do. Everybody has a role to play in helping to lift others.

II. HEEDING THE CALL

Service is the rent that you pay for room on this earth.
—Shirley Chisholm

Everyone can be great because everyone can serve.
—Martin Luther King, Jr.

I've learned that a community's wealth is not measured by how high the most gifted and able can rise, but by how far the most vulnerable are permitted to fall.
—John Records

There are many reasons why people are moved to volunteer. Some feel a spiritual calling to serve. Others respond to an imperative that is less specifically defined, but equally compelling. Still others have been inspired by the generosity of role models.

Yet, whatever the impetus, volunteers tend to share a common perception that, in giving of themselves, they are doing what they were "meant to do." The activity of giving feels both appropriate and necessary.

Brian Dixon

"It's the boy that wanted a warm jacket that got me into this."

Background

Brian Dixon was raised in Novato, California and graduated from Sacramento State University. He has been a mortgage broker in Novato since 1988 and has been a resident of Petaluma since 1993. His mother is a psychotherapist who had volunteered for Marin Suicide Prevention for many years and is also on the Board of a nonprofit in Marin. Brian has volunteered with many community service projects throughout his career, mostly involving helping children and needy families. Since his introduction to COTS, Brian transitioned from being a donor to a donor and a volunteer, mentoring in the Rent Right program. In 2005 he became the President of the COTS Board of Directors.

Thoughts on Volunteering and Service

I personally feel that if you're doing business in an area, you should commit some time to give back something to people who aren't as lucky as you are.

I'm not religious. I don't know where my need to help comes from. Maybe I just see how my work doesn't have a lot meaning in and of itself. If I lower someone's interest rate by ½% for their loan, that's great, but it doesn't really have a big effect on the world. I want to do something with a little more meaning.

How Brian Became Connected with COTS

About thirteen years ago, during the holiday season, I was out shopping for gifts at K-Mart and they had one of those gifting trees. There was a tag on it that said all a little boy wanted was a warm jacket for Christmas. I'll always remember that. I have never treated Christmas the same way since I saw it.

That year I took three or four of the tags and bought gifts for the people on the tree. It's the boy that wanted a warm jacket that got me into this. Ever since then, I don't buy gifts for my adult friends. What I do is write a list, give each person a dollar figure that I might have spent on them, write a check to COTS for that amount, and send each friend a note that a donation has been made in their name. I've been trying to get the people who buy me gifts to do the same for me, and it's catching on slowly but surely. Last Christmas, I got a thank-you note from COTS because someone had donated $200 in my name. I hope I see more of those down the road. Maybe I need to be more aggressive about letting people know that I would prefer receiving a note from COTS to getting a watch.

Why Brian Stays Connected with COTS

There are a lot of band-aids out there, but COTS is not a band-aid. It's helping the people that are down and out (for whatever reason) move on. That's why I've stayed. I see that it does push people to take steps, and I've seen the successes.

Mentoring for Rent Right

I've been the president of the COTS Board for the last couple of years. I've also been, for about four years, a mentor with the COTS Rent Right program, which is a 9-week course that helps individuals and families get all the tools, documents and skills they need to transition to independent housing. I had been a donor to COTS for over ten years, but I wanted to do more than just write a check. I'm a mortgage broker, so Rent Right was a perfect fit for me as I generally deal with different credit situations on a daily basis.

As a mentor, you're hooked up with two, three, or four clients who are taking the class. You're there to push them along and help them out with their projects and homework. You get on the phone each week and say "How's it going? Here's what you're supposed to be doing. Are you on track?" I think it does make a big difference. If that class was done without mentors, there'd probably be a higher drop-out rate.

One of their tasks involves writing letters, and I usually help them write the letters, as well as push them to make calls on their credit reports. I work with a lot of people on their credit reports, even if they're not my mentorees. It is always great to see a lot of familiar faces when I visit the Mary Isaak Center or our Family Shelter.

They had an art show at the Mary Isaak Center some time ago—because there are a lot of creative people there—and I actually bought a painting by a woman I had been working with in Rent Right. That painting hangs in my home office now.

I also stayed in touch with another one of my mentorees after he did the course. He ended up becoming a car salesman at Toyota and I bought my new car from him.

On Getting Involved in Volunteering

I tell people to do whatever they can, whether it's writing a check once in a while, donating some warm socks, or something else. Do what you can. Find what charity fits your life and what's important to you.

It's kind of like that shampoo commercial. You tell two friends, and they tell two friends, and they tell two friends. That's what I hope will happen with my holiday gift/donation idea, and maybe my friends will see that it feels good, and will need to tell other people about this. In fact, my thank-you card from COTS for that $200 donation in my name said, "See, someone's finally listening to you."

Tim Kellgren

"The church belongs wherever there's human need."

Background

Tim was raised in White Bear Lake, Minnesota (near Saint Paul), in a "normal suburban family." He had a younger sister and older brother. Both parents worked: his dad in the early computer industry, and his mom, during school hours, at the local drug store soda fountain and at the nursing home where Tim himself ended up working while in seminary. He remembers a wonderful childhood of outdoor play, in the neighborhood, in the woods, and at the lake down the street.

The family lived next to the church where Tim found his personal calling to be a minister. Though most of his role models were "negative," leading him to think he could do a better job if given the chance, the church was a place he felt accepted and affirmed. It was also a place where Tim's father had a "ministry" as the superintendent of the Sunday school.

Early Influences

Growing up in the church and hearing the message of the gospel, I ab- sorbed the idea that to be a Christian is to serve the world, that it is an essential part of following Jesus. After I graduated from St. Olaf and was in Luther Seminary in St. Paul, Minnesota, I spent a couple of summers in Chicago. I drove a Coca-Cola truck, which took me to the seedy, nitty-gritty parts of the city. It was very fascinating. This was in the '60s, and I spent a lot of time visiting different organizations, listening to speakers talking about urban renewal and justice. That was a very awakening time for me, seeing the reality of working in the community. The churches there were doing things.

I served churches in Minnesota and Illinois for a few years, and in 1977 came to California. Soon after I arrived here I was talking with a couple of other pastors in town. We began asking the question, "What are the needs in this community that aren't being met?" At that time we identified the fact that there was no subsidized housing for seniors. We decided to see if there was something we could do about it. None of us knew anything about how to build senior housing, but we knew how to take the first step; we began talking to people. Pretty soon some other people knew about what we were doing. We rounded up community support and invited other churches to participate. We ended up with a core group of seven or eight churches and their representatives, one of whom was an architect. We developed Petaluma Ecumenical Properties (PEP) Housing and step-by-step we began to build housing for seniors. It was an amazing project to work on, and eventually we did it. PEP now has over 200 apartments and continues to build more.

How Tim Got Involved with COTS

I remember trying to get a handle on the homeless situation and what we as a congregation could be doing, and realizing what a big task it was. Oftentimes people would stop by the office and ask for ten bucks or twenty bucks for a ride or for food, or to spend the night. I always regretted that I couldn't say to them, "Well, I won't give you ten dollars, but I'll help you change you life." So when Laure Reichek and Mary Isaak began COTS, and they were looking for places to have a shelter, the Methodist Church stepped forward first and said they could use the social hall for an evening shelter. Elim Lutheran Church, where I am the pastor now, had a rental house next door to our church, and when it became available, I asked our leadership team if they would consider making it available to COTS. It was most heartening. Without hesitation, they agreed. It was a small, scruffy little three-bedroom house. One night we had twenty-six people staying in it! That was the beginning, and then I got on the COTS Board of Directors. I think it was about 1988 or '89, pretty early in COTS' history.

I served on the Board for quite a while, at one point as President. I took some time off, realizing it was time for others to have a chance to participate, but then I came back to see what I could continue to learn. I feel like I'm part of COTS and that COTS is part of me. I want to stay around and see what more I can do to help the ministry that COTS is doing in the community. I keep finding new ways to do that.

COTS as Ministry

In a sense, I harbor a bit of jealousy because COTS has done so well. I think the work that COTS does is something that I would liked to have seen the churches do. The church belongs wherever there's human need—I think the church should have been serving the homeless long before COTS came along. But there isn't a single congregation in Petaluma large enough to do this. COTS has provided the structure for fifteen, twenty congregations or more to be part of this work, along with other folks who might not have been involved had it been specifically religious. An overarching vision like COTS has is important for a community the size of Petaluma, because a lot can happen when you bring in all kinds of resources as COTS has done. In a way, COTS has been the entity that has enabled ministry to happen, drawing out and coordinating all these different resources, allowing congregations and people of faith to come together and accomplish things together in a very creative, ecumenical, unity-building way. I'm delighted that lots of people from Elim have been part of it too. Now when someone comes and asks for ten bucks, I can say, "No, but I'll help you change your life," and bring them down to COTS.

During the early days when we used the rental at Elim, I was very in-volved in a hands-on way, as were many people in our congregation. The rental was just across the parking lot from the main building. People would mention that they had dropped off toilet paper or groceries—it was important to them to participate in a face-to-face way. I'll never forget the time all of the families turned up at one of our worship services. One woman stood before us and thanked everyone for making the facilities available and for all our support. It was important for the congregation to be touched that way by the people who were being helped.

Personal Challenges at COTS

When I was president there were some very difficult years financially. And personally, there's always been the challenge of meeting new folks who are in difficult circumstances, and being truly compassionate and open to seeing them as equals, as people who have as much to teach as receive.

Once I came to a meeting for the people who were sleeping at the Armory. John Records was addressing the whole group. There had been some problems, and he was trying to impress on them the need to be good citizens if they were going to participate in the program, and if the program was going to survive. As he talked, I kept moving closer and closer just to hear a little bit better, and I found myself standing behind some chairs. I moved in pretty close. Suddenly, the woman sitting on the chair in front of me just turned around and punched me in the stomach, catching me completely off-guard. I didn't fully understand what had happened, but after talking with John and some others, it became clear that here was a woman who had probably been abused by men, was fearful of men, and I had intruded into her space. I was too close.

It reminded me that this isn't a straight line kind of work; it's not just a do-gooder thing. We're dealing with people whose lives have been severely damaged. We have to respect their journey. It's not about me, it's about them and their healing. That can take a lot of different routes, and twists and turns, and we need to respond their real needs. This incident showed me that I was not particularly in tune with the folks that were there. It happened because I had overstepped a boundary. It underscored the need for me to really be attentive to what's going on in a situation.

The Meaning of Service

For me, service comes out of my religious and spiritual background. As I read the New Testament, and try to discern and clarify who Jesus is, I see in him someone calling us to give our lives. We have been given incredible gifts, especially being recipients of all the benefits of this particular culture that we live in. It's essential to our spiritual growth, it's essential to being human, to make our lives available for the sake of other people. I just finished studying the Gospel of Mark with a group of the congregation. In that Gospel, Jesus is, over and over again, emphasizing to his followers that life is about giving ourselves away. And the disciples never get it—even at the end, they're asking questions like, "Who's going to be the greatest in the kingdom of God? Me or my brother?" "Can I sit at your left hand or your right hand in the kingdom?" They just never come round and get what Jesus was talking about. And it's such a contemporary gospel, because in the Christian community we continue to be mesmerized by status and position and wealth. But He just keeps pulling us to a life of giving ourselves to the world, and telling us that is the way life is best lived. In some ways it's almost selfish to serve, because it is the way to a life that's most meaningful and fulfilling.

In a sense, we have to unclench our fist and open our hand, which releases and offers what we have to the world, and then our hand is open to receive back. Whereas if our fists are clenched, holding on to what we have, we can neither give nor receive. Jesus talks about "emptying ourselves" and that's the same thing. We pour ourselves out. And then we're empty to receive and be filled by that which is much deeper and more profound and transformative and filled with love. It's true on a much deeper level than we ever felt possible. We really find ourselves being transformed in ways that we could not have expected or directed or anticipated.

There is a connection between service and surrender. In the courses I teach, I talk about surrender as one of Christ's principles. It's not about when or how we are able to live a life of surrender; surrender is what we're *created* to do. And so, again, when we hang onto our own lives, we restrict the natural flow of God's energy and healing and wholeness into ourselves, and into the world around us that needs us to surrender. Different people seem to be able to surrender at earlier stages in life—those who become saints, if you will, in any religious spiritual tradition, often have been able to surrender quite early, so they have lot of time to be filled with God. For others, it takes some years. And we each have to struggle with that to discern what ways we can best serve.

There are all kinds of people working and volunteering for COTS who have a variety of gifts. You need the whole package. There's a comment from Mother Theresa: "We can do no great things, but we can do small things with great love." When you trust that God will take care of Heaven, and God knows what He is doing, then you follow Jesus and become Christ-like, which means giving yourself away.

Roger Kirkpatrick

"To make sense of existence on this planet, one must realize that we are all connected."

Background

Roger Kirkpatrick is the Associate Executive Director and Chief Operations Officer at COTS. His involvement and interests support every part of COTS' work.

Childhood

I was born in Calgary, Alberta, Canada a long time ago. My mother and father were children of the Depression. My father had to drop out of high school in the 10th grade to help support his family. He started out as an office boy in an oil company and ended up in Latin America at age 19. He worked extremely hard and by age 21 was in charge of financial and operational auditing for all of Columbia.

He was a very generous man, always there to support a family member. When I think of my father, I think of *character*. I think of a person who accepted responsibility for himself and his family, who worked hard and never complained.

My father was very intelligent and very rational. Honesty and integrity meant a lot to him. He believed in treating people very fairly. If I could fault him for anything, it might be that he didn't relax as much as he should have.

My mother was different. She was gentle and kind. I never heard her say one negative thing about anybody. She had a very open, warm, loving personality. She was a religious woman who spent a lot of time reading the Bible, and she would talk to me about passages from the Bible. Her message was of love. I don't recall her ever talking about what I call the sterner aspects of religion, such as everlasting punishment. It was more about gentleness, love, compassion, and charity.

My mother was a quiet, retiring person who stayed close to home. Her charity occurred on a one-to-one basis.

They were very different people, but they had a successful marriage that lasted over 50 years. My father continued to live for about four years after my mother passed away, and I remember him saying that he missed her terribly and wanted to be with her. I saw him gradually let go of this world in order to join with her again, spiritually.

It is very clear to me that each of them lives on through me, which I feel very good about. I carry them with me.

Growing up, I was good at athletics. I was a natural at football. I was good in track and field. I was good at basketball. I had strength and speed and agility. I also loved the outdoors, and spent many weekends in the Everglades. I became a passionate snake-hunter! I wouldn't kill them but I would catch them. That became my absolute passion.

After a slow start, I eventually became a pretty good student. I had a good mind, but I had what we now call attention deficit hyperactivity disorder (ADHD). I had a hard time concentrating, and a very hard time sitting still. People thought I had a learning disability. The way I tended to handle that was to withdraw, which didn't help things. I spent a lot of time alone. That's why nature was so appealing to me. I became very independent and self-reliant, which eventually served me well.

In any event, my innate intelligence allowed me to eventually do well in high school and get into a good college, Northwestern.

The University Years

I did well at Northwestern in spite of the ADHD. By then, I had learned to be very organized and disciplined. I put in a lot of time studying, to the point where I can say that I never walked out of a test thinking I could have done better if I had only studied harder. I majored in English Literature. History and philosophy were also areas I was interested in.

At the end of my junior year, my dad asked me, "What are you going to do next?" I said, "I don't know." And he said, "Well, have you thought about law school?" I said, "I don't know if I want to be a lawyer." And he said, "Well, you don't have to be a lawyer. I work with a lot of businessmen who have law degrees and they're wonderful ... the way their minds work." That's what got me thinking about law. I decided that I had to move to a place a lot warmer than Chicago, so I applied to law school at Stanford.

At the end of law school, it became very clear to me that I didn't want to practice law. I was very interested in business and management, but when I interviewed for positions, I learned that my law degree didn't open up any doors that weren't already open to me when I graduated from Northwestern.

So, back to school I went, applying to Wharton graduate school and ending up with a degree in finance and accounting. This time around, the combination of the law degree and business degree were really valuable, and I had no lack of opportunity to interview for a variety of interesting positions.

Professional Life

My first assignment after graduation from business school took me to Wichita, Kansas. I had joined a consulting business and was asked to develop a going-concern valuation for a company about to be acquired. The company being acquired was Lear Jet Industries. I was 28 years old and had never worked as a professional consultant before. The president of Lear Jet and his wife picked me up and took me out to dinner. I remember that when the president went to the bathroom, his wife looked at me and said, "You look very young to be doing this sort of thing. How long have you been doing it?" I said, "This is my first assignment!" For the rest of the dinner, by the look on her face, I could see she desperately wanted to tell her husband just who they were dealing with!

I worked in consulting for four years. I developed a specialty as a problem solver, working with companies in financial trouble. I would work with the president to develop a sense of direction for the company. What are our strengths? What are our core competencies? What are the things we don't do well? We would develop a plan for getting the company out of trouble, and I would assist in restructuring the finances of the company in order to execute that strategy.

At the end of the four years, I decided to focus on developing my management skills. Since I was working in a bank at the time, the best opportunity to do this was in what's called back-office operations, which include things like check processing, money transfers and so forth. This end of banking was people-intensive, and by working in this area I developed leadership and management skills. I was Division Head and reported to an Executive Vice President of the bank. I had about 1,000 people working for me and an annual operating budget of approximately $12 million. I was now in my mid-30's.

As a manager, I believed in emphasizing the positive—allowing people to participate, emphasizing good two-way communication, and treating people with respect. Also, I believed in leading by example. I never asked others to do things I wasn't ready to do myself. This approach worked well for me; I received an extremely positive evaluation of my leadership and management style. It was very meaningful to me that I had been able to work in a high-performance environment and manage according to my values at the same time. The pride I took in this accomplishment made me realize I was more interested in helping to create a better world than in acquiring power, status, and money.

I see a lot of good in our economic system—in good products and services, meaningful jobs, work environments where people are respected, people being able to afford decent homes and health care, and companies behaving as responsible corporate citizens (including fulfilling their environmental responsibilities). I believe that economics and good citizenship can go together. But we have to realize that life is about a lot more than things. It's about people, the spiritual quality of our lives, and being good citizens, not just as individuals but as communities and nations. It can all fit together. I have always been committed to products or services that I could take pride in. I wouldn't try to fix a cigarette company.

Volunteering

When my oldest son reached the age of 7 or 8, I got involved with youth sports. I coached soccer and baseball and eventually helped to coordinate youth sports programs. Working with children turned out to be a wonderful opportunity to do exciting things outside of the work environment. Coaching sports allowed me to teach children the values of teamwork and healthy competition. I also enjoyed the positive impact it had on the parents. For example, giving single moms a respite from their busy days or giving parents a chance to see their children experience personal growth.

I had become increasingly aware of the plight of the least fortunate people in our society, particularly when I lived in Santa Monica, which has a large homeless population. I was able to witness people's efforts to do good, such as women who would prepare and serve hot food to homeless people out of the backs of their vehicles on a regular basis. I was very impressed by the power of individual effort to make a real difference. I started to think that I had a lot of skills that might be brought to bear to solve the problem of homelessness, and I went looking for an opportunity to apply them.

Working at COTS

I was interviewing for the position of Executive Director of Habitat for Humanity and John Records was assisting in the interviewing process. They didn't hire me, but the next day, I received an email from John offering to give me a tour of the COTS family center. I started out as a volunteer and that led to working there.

I'm involved in fundraising, operations, and program development, but I have an intellectual, emotional, and spiritual connection with the entire organization. I particularly enjoy opportunities to work directly with clients, such as mentoring in the Rent Right program, helping people create new lives for themselves.

In retrospect, I realize that an important part of what I enjoyed about my business career was teaching and coaching people. I enjoyed helping people achieve their potential, encouraging them to do their best, and showing them how they could succeed in business and live by worthwhile values at the same time.

Business people start with a vision and translate this vision into a detailed process for solving problems or pursuing opportunities. There are many activities in the nonprofit world that also require these skills. One example that comes to mind involves the federally-mandated effort to develop a Homeless Management Information System, which is a big challenge for Sonoma County and its human services agencies. Project planning and management skills apply here. A business person's perspective can be very valuable in the nonprofit environment. It boils down to how we can make the most effective use of our resources.

When I worked with companies in trouble, my motto was that survival is an appropriate short-run goal but not an appropriate long-run goal. Organizations need to thrive over the long run. By analogy, at COTS we help homeless people survive in the short run by meeting their basic needs for shelter and food, and then help them thrive by providing resources for people who are ready to change their lives.

Nonprofit work is much more collaborative than most endeavors in the business world. There's more sharing and listening, and there's a big payoff when everyone helps everybody else. There are no politics, gossip, or backstabbing. There is none of that at COTS. It's clear that at COTS we are here for each other.

I have to say it's John Records' leadership that creates this environment. Leaders attract people who share and respond to the leader's values. We emphasize resiliency here, the inherent good in all of us and the innate strength that we all possess. If we see a deficiency, we don't dwell on the negative but, rather, focus on the positive.

For me, a story that represents what we're about involves two clients that I mentored in our Rent Right course. They both made it clear at the outset that they didn't want to be there. As the course progressed, their reluctance turned into begrudging participation, and, eventually, into enthusiastic participation. They went from being self-absorbed to becoming aware of others, to saying "thank you" or "I'm sorry" when it was appropriate, and even expressing humor. When we had our Rent Right graduation ceremony, as they got their diplomas I was struck by the fact that they showed the same kind of pride that someone graduating from a prestigious university would show. I remember how proud I was of them and how gratified I felt to be doing this work.

I feel that to make sense of existence on this planet, one must realize that we are all connected. So when we take care of our neighbors, we take care of ourselves. By serving others, we help to create a better world for each one of us.

I remember when I first checked out the COTS website, I came across the statement that "greatness in a community is not measured by how high its most talented people rise but how willing the community is to let its least fortunate people fall." COTS and Petaluma are carrying out the will of the community in helping the least fortunate to not fall any further and to rise when they are ready to help themselves. Our community is not just people who work in government–it's congregations who provide shelter, high schools who raise funds, women who make quilts for children, bookstores and grocery stores who share their profits. We reflect what is good about this community.

Marge Popp

"I serve the needy and the greedy. . . .
I haven't had a bad day in twenty-five years."

Background

Marge grew up in Petaluma during the great depression of the 1930s. She attended St. Vincent's Grammar and High School. After high school, she worked at a local creamery for 40 years until she was laid off when the company was sold. In 1982, she began volunteering for the Petaluma Kitchen three days a week and, 25 years later, she continues to cook for the Kitchen, starting her workdays at 7:00 a.m.

Discovering Service: The Depression

I was about eleven years old. There were about 4,000 people living in Petaluma at the time. Back in those days, in the 30s, my mother used to tell me not to let anybody in the house. We weren't worried about tramps coming in the house uninvited; nobody locked their doors. They knocked, and if someone answered, fine, and if they didn't, they went away.

But when there were tramps at the back door, I would always invite 'em in. I didn't mean to disobey my mother, but people were hungry, and I wanted to make sure that they ate. We had a back porch, and I would say, "Mama, he's hungry." And she'd make a sandwich, and I'd bring it out to them, and then they'd leave. Nothing special—it would be a cheese sandwich or an egg sandwich or peanut butter and jelly. Nobody objected.

And each one, if they enjoyed the meal, would make some kind of a mark on the door casing, which was very interesting, like half a sunrise and the railroad tracks. The marks meant that this house would be kind to you. And then other people—hobos, we would call them in those days—would come by and see these marks, and know, "This is a good house to stop at." Maybe what I do now actually started back then.

Over time I got busy with high school and the visits tapered off. Then came the war, and then there were no tramps—they all went to work in the defense factories.

A Call to Service: The Petaluma Kitchen

Western Creameries, where I worked for forty years, laid off staff in November of 1981. There was a recession at the time and no one was hiring 57-year-old ladies for anything. Employers wanted the younger people. I stayed home for about a month, and I thought, "I've got to do something. I'm awfully bored just doing nothing." So I went by the Kitchen one day, stopped in, and helped make sandwiches.

I began volunteering at the Kitchen in February of 1982. The Kitchen had started in December of 1981 after a flood affected homes in the area. It was set up to help people who'd lost their homes in the flood. People who didn't have relatives to stay with would come down to the Kitchen to have a meal.

And then, one by one, different people would drift in and I never paid attention to whether they were homeless or not, because they were looking for a meal. And to this day, it doesn't make a difference to me if they're down and out, or just need companionship. I like to say, I serve the needy and the greedy.

The numbers grew to two hundred and seventy-five people coming in. We volunteers cleaned bathrooms, swept floors, emptied garbage cans, cooked and served, put food away, and kept making sandwiches. Then, one day, the lady who ran the Kitchen came to me and said, "I'm quitting so I can go back to school. You're going to be the cook." That's how I became the lead cook.

I didn't know how I could put together a meal for so many people with an odd supply of ingredients that changed every day, depending on donations. A man named Dennis Maloney, a daring Irishman who also volunteered in the kitchen, said, "If you don't know how to cook just start throwing things together." I mean, I wouldn't put salt instead of sugar in the pudding, but that advice got me going.

There was also a sweet and kind German lady, Hettie Sweeney, who had been there before I was. She knew how to cook and I didn't, so she would help me too. One time we had some sauce that was very, very salty—how it happened, I don't know. I probably put something wrong in it. So she said, "Add some raw potatoes to it, and it'll take out the salt flavor." And of course she was right.

Never Take the Credit and Never Take the Blame

Well, round here it's not like a restaurant; you just have basic stuff to work with. You make stews or a roast or a ham, none of these soup-plate type things that big restaurants would make. We have salt, pepper, garlic, thyme, rosemary, but no exotic things. We cook with whatever we got. So, for the main course, if it only calls for, say, three cans of corn and three cans of tomatoes, and I have eight cans of corn and one of tomatoes, all the cans go in and that's it.

The volunteers and I prepare everything. I ask people, "Please cut this," or "Please do that," and I oversee the whole thing, but I'm right in there working too. Sometimes when I ask the volunteers to do something, they wonder, "How's it going to come out?" I say, "Don't worry. I never take the credit and I never take the blame." That's my motto.

Almost every day there's something unusual. I'll make a pasta sauce and it may have pesto sauce in it, it may have spaghetti sauce, it may have sour cream or cottage cheese. When you mix them all up, it comes out all right! You have to make it up as you go, depending on what you have. I even put jam in it once. Not on purpose, but it came out fine! I think it was peach jam—it gave it a little bit of a tart crunch.

We plan meals by picking the meat that we have the most of. Whatever we got goes into the stew: vegetables, potatoes, whatever. We used to get a lot of lunch meat, so I thought, "Well, I don't know how it'll come out, but I'll fix something." So we fried potatoes and onions, and added the cut-up lunch meat to it, and made a, well, whatever you want to call it, and it seemed to go over good, and we fix it once in a while when we have enough lunch meat.

A lot of times I'll fix what we call "tallorini" when we have a lot of corn. Tallorini is a mixture of corn, tomatoes, olives, hamburger and noodles. We make it in big, big pans, so it's like a very large casserole, enough to feed 125 people.

One time a volunteer, Terry, brought in raisins and somehow or other I put these raisins in the soup. It was a mistake! But nobody objected to them, and Terry couldn't get over that. Since then I've found out that there are some soups that are supposed to have raisins in them. So-- I don't take the blame, and I don't take the credit. That's the end of that.

Lessons Learned: The Good with the Bad

A nice young man who'd been coming in regularly to eat stopped me one day before he came in, and he said, "I want to thank you. You've been so nice to me. And you know what? I just got a job!" And I said, "Well, that's wonderful. But don't you stop coming in to eat. Come in to eat and save your money, until you have at least a couple of month's salary put away, and then you can *still* continue eating here. Or, if you want to, you can donate here some day."

Of course, we get a lot of scruff 'n' roughs too. The Kitchen now has managers that are good about handling the not-so-nice people. But there are very few bad apples. You do get one or two who aren't so nice. But you gotta just overlook those, because a lot of times they can't help it. There's a lady with Tourette's syndrome who comes to the Kitchen and she's a good example of someone who can't help herself, though her behavior can be kind of upsetting for people who don't know her condition. If she's got jewelry on, I call her "Ma'am." If she comes in with a derby hat on, I call her "Sir." And she doesn't object to either.

Most of the people that come in are real down-and-out, and they're all kind, they're all polite, and most of them say "Thank you, it was good" or "Thanks for the dinner." They're very, very nice. I can't engage in much conversation while they're going through the food line, but I want to know people's names, so I can say, "Hello there, John." I think if you call some-body by their name, they feel a little more important than they do if you just say hello.

Some stand in the corner and eat. Maybe they feel safer with their back to the corner, or they want to be ready to get out if the cops come. Maybe they've never been taught that it's nice to sit down and eat. If I get a chance I go over to them and say, "Hi, we like all our guests to be seated while they eat." Some of them will give me a dirty look, and some will sit down. I don't insist on anything; I just ask them once and that's it.

I try to work with people. One man had a terrible abscessed tooth, and I kept asking him if he got it taken care of yet. He couldn't chew so I wouldn't give him any heavy stuff, like meat. I tried to give him vegetables and stuff like that. Then he got his tooth fixed, and he is now fine. And there are a couple ladies that have had heart problems that can hardly eat anything. We've had to call the ambulance for them. I've seen some terrible sad things.

But when the little kids thank you, and older people come in and say they had a good meal, or "You made me feel good," it's lovely. Like Willie. He was a nice kid. He ate at the Kitchen for about six months. All of a sudden, after those six months, we didn't see Willie anymore. You can't keep track of people because a lot of times you don't know their real names. Then one day his mother brought in his first paycheck, as a donation to the Kitchen! Now that was really nice. When she brought that paycheck in, that was a big thank you.

There was another time that two men dressed as motorcyclists came in. They didn't eat, and they looked different to me, but nothing was said or done. They came in a couple of other times and ate; I never asked anything about them, or said "Why are you here?" because that's not our place. And then three or four weeks later they came in again and gave us a check for ten thousand dollars. I found out that they were from the band called the Grateful Dead. They never said anything at the time. They just handed us the check, and then they finished eating and left. There was no time to thank them.

Challenges and Inviting Others to Service

I always try to make meals more appetizing. The ladies I work with are all very friendly, very kind, and willing to work. They're very intelligent people. We've got one lady that's a photographer, and another that's a lawyer, and another that's a schoolteacher. All types of people come in, and we all have one purpose: to contribute something and to do something useful. One lady is great at using the tops of beets and the tops of chard, so I said, "Well, I'll put that in the spaghetti sauce." And we cut it up and it gives it a nice flavor.

We have men volunteering too. Some men work as dishwashers. My husband comes in and does some of the heavy work. One man, Tony Mazzamuto, is a professional chef and he comes in and adds his talents to our cooking.

Bill Rogers is a friend of my husband's and mine. I talked him into coming down to help out at the Kitchen. I said, "It's a good place to work, plenty of coffee, have a lot of fun—why don't you come down and try it?" And he did. And he's still there! He has volunteered at the Kitchen for eleven years now.

About Service and Advice to Others on Service

Just try to be kind and helpful. That's all. Don't be grouchy! I want to be happy all the time. I don't want to make people unhappy, and I don't want to be unhappy.

Service to me is things like keeping the place clean, keeping the cupboards clean, keeping the drawers free from pieces of lettuce and crumbs that get in them. I like to run a neat ship. I was never in the Navy, but other volunteers call me—"Military Police."

I want to give to people that are in a tough spot. Sure, it makes me feel good. Some people say that I'm motherly, but I don't feel like a mother! I like to be treated kindly, too. I haven't had a bad day in twenty-five years. For me, it's the challenge to do better that keeps me going. You should see some of the things that come in! Some things aren't too presentable when they arrive. I want to make good food, keep the place clean, and just make life a little better for people.

Susan Rodkin

"There are constant calls for help."

Background

Susan Rodkin grew up in Camas, Washington, a mill town on the Ore-
gon/Washington border. Her mother, daughter of Danish immigrants, is one of twelve
children. Susan has approximately forty-five first cousins on her mother's side.

Both of Susan's parents were models of service. Her mother was a secretary at the
Lutheran church, where Susan has been a member all her life. Every day after school, she
would walk to the church, five blocks away, and be in the office with her mom, folding
bulletins, running errands, and scooting along the floor under the pews.

Susan currently is an elementary school principal. Susan served for two years as the
Chairperson of the Board of Directors at COTS. She continues to attend COTS events,
and is active at the rotational family shelter.

Learning Service from the Family

My parents are eighty-eight and eighty-seven, and they live in an as-
sisted living situation in Washington State. To this day they live a life of
service. For years, they had a regular routine during the week, going to visit
"old people," bringing food, comfort, conversation. They worked in the
local shelter, the local thrift store; they volunteered as reading tutors, each
mentoring one child in the schools.

My parents taught by example. They demonstrated that we were one
part of a great whole, that caring for one another was the most important

part of our lives. They also taught that what we were given in our lives, who we really are, was because of our all-loving God. We are able to love because God first loved us. I can remember childhood songs: "Love is something that if you give it away, you end up having more." "Love is like a magic penny: you hold it tight, and you won't have any; lend it spend it, you'll have so many they'll roll all over the floor."

I'm number three of four siblings. I have two older brothers and a younger sister. My oldest brother, Jim, is a professor at Idaho State University; he's Dean of the Health Sciences Department there. He's involved in health education, ways to improve life for people in the community. He's politically active in the State of Idaho, working with groups who are involved in AIDS research. He's very attentive to nutrition concerns, a real leader in his area. He and my sister-in-law, Georgia, are also very active in their church and community. They're incredibly giving, vibrant people. My brother is a role model for me, there's no doubt about it. He's a very charismatic person; loving, but very low-key and humble.

My second brother, Dan, and his family moved to the Bay Area about four years ago. He was an executive with Crown-Zellerbach. When Georgia-Pacific purchased it a year ago, he was, as they say, golden parachuted, so now he gives his time to raising his second family. He's a stay-at-home dad with young children, an incredibly generous person.

My sister is three years younger. She's also in education. She works in teacher support. My sister is one of the best examples of a person who is able to see the beauty in everyone and bring out the best in others. She's an incredible leader. People flock to her. She's a developer of others, a very giving, loving person. I have incredible siblings, I really do.

One of my very early memories is of my maternal grandfather, Nis Nissen Hagensen, who emigrated from Denmark to the Pacific Northwest. He was a farmer, but that was not enough to support a family, so he worked in the paper mill too. My mom has many, many memories of him taking food that my grandmother had canned, or meat or eggs from the farm, and delivering the food to families close by who didn't have anything, who had young children or children who were sick. My grandfather had very little, but he was so amazingly considerate of other people.

Susan's Involvement with COTS

It was very early. I got involved through Tim Kellgren. Tim was an incredible role model for me as my pastor, my counselor, and just a great friend. The church owned a small house, which was used as one of the first shelters for COTS families. I became involved with helping to get the house ready. Rich, my husband, helped as well, providing meals. Then, I gradually became more involved, spending nights with the families at our church, bringing food, playing with the children. It just seemed like the opportunity was there, an open door. So I stepped through that door.

Then Tom Joynt started talking with me about joining the COTS Board. I became the Board's chair for a couple of years, after Tom's tenure ended in 2002.

The Rotational Shelter

I no longer serve on the Board, but I still help out at my church's rotational shelter. I help with meals and transportation and I still stay overnight when I can. My husband and I are financial supporters too.

There isn't always room at the COTS Family Center, especially during winter when the demand is high. So the churches step in and do as much as they can. The rotational shelter gives families a temporary place to stay.

Often, when I've stayed overnight, I've connected deeply with the moms and dads and children. One time I talked to a young woman who was a sophomore in high school. We just sat at the kitchen table at my church, and she talked about how much trauma her family had been through, and how much stigma was attached to being homeless, and how COTS had been able to intervene for her family. This was a sixteen-year-old girl talking! She told me that COTS helped her family realize that there was a support system for them, some stability that could help them get their lives back in order.

She was grateful that she could sit there and do her homework, and have her belongings in one place. It wasn't ideal, it wasn't a home, but the support that COTS was providing—a place to do laundry, career counseling for her mom and dad—it felt like a lot.

Sitting there and having an intimate conversation with this girl, and later talking with her parents, I began to really get a picture of what they'd been through. I followed that family and I'm happy to say they were very successful in finding housing.

Another family came through with five children. As an educator, I was able to work with some of the children in that family. They're doing well now too; they have a home.

Those personal connections have made me so grateful for the work of COTS. It gives me so much beyond what I give. I get back a hundred times what I put into the work. I feel so blessed. COTS lets me touch my neighbors' lives, right here in our community of Petaluma.

I want to ease the pain people feel in their lives, but it's also a spiritual journey for me. Life is painful, and we all experience that, but we bring joy to life though our relationships and caring. That's what gives everything else meaning. How could one go through life without noticing and caring and wanting to ease the lives of others?

Personal Challenges with COTS

One challenge has been trying to be an ambassador and educator about homelessness. People hold stereotypical views of why homeless people are homeless: They think homeless people should just be able to get with the program, pull themselves up by their bootstraps, get a job, and find housing. But it's not that simple. The roots of homelessness, the conditions that cause a person's life to go in that direction, could happen to any of us. It's a very fine line between living in a nice home and facing a life on the streets. I don't want to ever be complacent about the blessings I enjoy.

Early one morning at the rotational shelter, I was visiting with one of the clients—a young man, in his mid-thirties, whom I really liked. He talked to me about his family. He'd been in business with his father, and still was. He was going that morning to work with his father. His wife was so hopeful about housing that she stopped every day to try to make contact with the developer of the place they were looking at moving into. She'd stop every day, and the man wasn't there, and he wasn't there, and he wasn't there. And she finally got his number, and she called. He said he'd been aware of her coming to the site and that he was going to make them a priority. Both of those people were so hopeful. I didn't ask, but I had to wonder what had happened with them? Where had things fallen apart?

Beliefs About Service

Basically I'm a child of God, and everything that I have is not mine, but it's mine to share—my self, my time and my resources. I'm a very optimistic person. My philosophy is that if there's anything I can do to ease the suffering or brighten the day of another person—whether it be in a tangible or intangible way—then that's a blessing for that day.

What COTS Means to Susan

COTS makes a difference in the lives of people who lack many of the physical and psychological comforts they need. It's a loving organization that gives people a real chance to get what they need in life. It's also research-based and uses tried and true strategies to help people get back on their feet and on with their lives.

I would invite others to see the opportunities that are available, that present themselves each and every day, to reach out to others—to their neighbors, to their families. I think it's important to start with the people that we are most intimately involved with, and to reach out from there. I would encourage everyone to look for ways to make a difference. There are constant calls for help.

There's so much more I could do. I'm not really putting my life on the line. I'm just a regular person doing regular things. I have a lot of room to grow. I'm excited about the work of COTS. It's great to be on this ride.

John Sedlander

"You become a different person . . ."

Background

John grew up in Detroit, Michigan. He attended the University of Michigan, where he received his Master's degree in Business and then spent the next thirty years working for corporations, "enhancing shareholder equity," as he likes to say. His career path spanned a wide range of roles with several different companies. His last position prior to joining COTS was with SOLA Optical in Petaluma as Distribution Manager; he also served as Manager of Financial Planning and Controller for SOLA. After many years as a volunteer, John left the corporate world to join COTS as Director of Operations for three years. After his "nest emptied" at home, John and his wife Ellen returned to San Francisco to live, and John took a senior management position in a nonprofit there.

Thoughts on Volunteering

I come from a family of volunteers. My dad volunteered for everything from tutoring illiterate adults, to serving on boards, to raising money for social service organizations. My parents volunteered partly for their own enjoyment, but also because it was the right thing to do. I picked up on that. When I was young, I volunteered at the church. And I have been volunteering ever since.

The church our family belonged to was the obvious place to volunteer. I was also an active member of the Boy Scouts, an Eagle Scout. I disagree with some of their policies now, but it was a fine organization and it got me outdoors. One award that I was going for with Boy Scouts and with church required 150 hours of volunteer work. So I did a lot of window washing and folding bulletins, and I also took part in activities around the school, working on events and Homecoming floats.

Why He Continues to Volunteer

I think there are a couple of reasons. I have a sense of duty about this.

Any organization that I get involved in wants me to be the treasurer. That might have to do with my financial background. I resisted this for a long time. But after a while I realized that I couldn't fight it anymore. It was my calling in life. I looked around at these organizations I was part of and realized that they were filled with good-hearted people who for the most part had little idea about how to balance books. If it was going to get done, I would need to do it.

So I spent years as Treasurer and Finance Committee Chair at Elim Lutheran Church. I'm on the board of the Old Adobe School District partly because of my financial expertise. I produce the financial statements for COTS; I was the treasurer for many years. I just find myself there and I'm comfortable with that spot.

Then again, if I'm going to do volunteer work, why not do something I enjoy? So I spend a lot of time coaching kids' soccer because I love playing soccer with the kids. I also like to sing. I love music, so why not sing in the choir? There are a lot more things that need to be done than there are people to do them.

I think it makes sense, though I do some things out of duty, to pick things I like *and* am good at. Being on an advisory committee is important but not always inspirational.

How He Came into Contact with COTS

I came into contact with COTS through a good friend of mine, Pastor Tim Kellgren. This must have been in the early nineties and he invited me out to lunch to propose that I join the COTS Board of Directors. I didn't know much about COTS, but by the end of the lunch I had accepted his offer and I ended up picking up the tab for lunch on top of it all!

At first, my involvement was minimal. I would just come to meetings, and gradually, as COTS does, it pulled me in more and more. I became involved in the finances. Then I got involved in the Sunday morning stays at the family shelter. I remember, a couple of times when we still had the Armory, spending the night there like a homeless person, to get the feel of it, the taste and feel and texture of it.

Around that time, my job at SOLA Optical was coming to an end. The last year was probably the most difficult; we were closing down eight locations and creating two new ones, and laying off over a hundred people. We did it with respect and gratitude, and I was amazed that people worked hard for us even up to the last day. After that I could have stayed with the company, but I would have had to move to San Diego. My plan was to instead take six months off and hike and spend some time in the outdoors, then find another job. But COTS' plan was for me to start work immediately. So I had one week off and plunged in. I accepted this job and I've really enjoyed it.

Role at COTS

We have two goals here. In the corporate world, it all comes down to the bottom line. Despite any "values statements" corporations come up with, the overriding value is to make as much money as you can and get the stock price up, and all the statements they make about customers and employees and suppliers are subservient to that.

At COTS we're here to help change our clients' lives for the better, and everything we do is directed at that. Much of our work is a free gift to people without expectations. We give somebody a nutritious lunch. We let somebody take a shower so they can look and feel better. We might ask, but we don't demand anything in return. Finding the right balance in that regard is a real challenge, because we have limited resources. So what services should be part of a contract and how much should be a free gift? There's a certain creative tension in that.

Challenges and Growth with COTS

One of the challenges that I find hard is when people's values don't align with ours. An example would be people in the neighborhood who really object to our presence in a mean-spirited way. That to me just seems so selfish. Maybe if I could put myself in their shoes I might feel a similar way… but I do put myself in their shoes and I know I wouldn't feel that way.

So how have I grown in that? I take it less personally and say that is how they feel, and this is how I feel and this is my job, so I will do the best job I can to respect them and not internalize their venomous comments. I have to be patient, not infinitely patient, but I have to listen and respond appropriately, and that's a continual challenge. That challenge is going to be with us for a long time in this field.

Another challenge is juggling the scarce resources that we have to work with. If you need something in the for-profit world, you just order it. Here, we never have enough people; we never have enough money; we never have enough space. And that's the way it's always going to be, and I end up feeling inadequate because I can't do it all. I just can't get this job done. I don't have enough time, I don't have enough staff, and the demands are so big. We keep coming up with new ideas of things we need to be doing, and more people come to our door. They're hurt and broken and we just do what we can and sometimes it's not enough. I do everything I can personally, and it's not enough.

A Particularly Sweet Moment

It was in the Petaluma Kitchen. A group of schoolchildren had come over to sing Christmas carols for us. The kitchen is usually a pretty raucous place but it really stilled down to listen to these sweet children. The kids came in and stood at one end of the dining room, and began singing Christmas carols. At the other end of the room were the collection of folks who show up at the Kitchen for lunch every day, a pretty weather-beaten crowd. I was watching the kids, but at one point I turned around to look at the crowd to see how they were reacting to the children's singing.

A whole bunch of these old homeless guys and women were singing along with "Silent Night." Some had tears in their eyes. I thought, "Wow, you forget that they know the words to 'Silent Night' too, but they probably haven't sung them in a long time." It was just a sweet moment.

Philosophy

My philosophy keeps changing and it's hard to articulate, but one of my beliefs is that a life well lived is a life of service to the greater good. There's a Hindu hymn that was supposedly Gandhi's favorite:

> *They are the real lovers of God who feel others' sorrow as their own.*
> *When they perform selfless service, they are humble servants of the Lord.*
> *Respecting all, despising none, they are pure in thought, word and deed.*
> *Blessed is the mother of such a child;*
> *In their eyes the Divine Mother shines in every woman they see.*
> *They are always truthful and even minded, never coveting others' wealth,*
> *Free of selfish attachments, ever in tune with the holy name.*
> *Their bodies are like sacred shrines in which the Lord of love is seen.*
> *Free from greed, anger, and fear, these are the real lovers of God.*

So to me that says it all. I'd like to live like that. Working in a place like this lines up pretty well with that precept.

What Service Means to John

Service is doing something you do for someone else, for their benefit. You could be motivated to serve others for your own satisfaction, and to some extent we all are. We get some positive feedback, for example. It's not all just sweaty grunt work. You think to yourself, "That was good" or "That felt good." I don't do this work for compliments, but they are a nice benefit.

I think there's a difference between the service itself and why you do it. I think you can be selfishly motivated to give good service. You may have some hope of getting something back. At COTS, we serve people and hope that their decisions align with ours, and then we can help them make a change. But if they don't, they don't.

Advice to Others on Volunteering and Service

My advice would be that if you think this is a good thing (doing some service for others) even if you find it difficult or you don't have time (because none of us have time) then you should do it anyway and make a commitment to serve for a period of time. The repetition and the doing of it somehow enable you to continue on.

If you just do it because it's convenient or has an immediate emotional payoff, you probably won't spend a lot of time at it. It's kind of like spiritual practices. Sometimes you just do them anyway even if you don't feel like it. The repetition over time has great value and sinks into who you are as a person. And you become a different person because of that repetition and service.

Sure, there are times where you wish you didn't have to coach soccer. There are times you wish you didn't have to go to choir rehearsal. There are times when it's pretty inconvenient to show up and deliver food for Food for Families on Saturday morning. You'd rather sleep in. But, if you keep doing it, your whole self becomes more evolved, and it becomes easier and more natural.

Bill White

"Giving is the embodiment of love."

Background

Bill White and his wife Pat founded Basin Street Properties, a commercial property development company based in Petaluma. Bill was raised in New Jersey. Bill's father commuted to New York and worked long hours, so Bill rarely saw him on weekdays. In spite of that, Bill had a very strong family life, with one older sister. His father, a huge fan of history and the New York Giants baseball team, passed away when Bill was 17. Bill, who came to California during his service in the Navy, credits his parents for giving him a strong sense of personal responsibility and hard work. He returned to the East Coast to complete his education and then came back to California in 1970. He and Pat settled in west Marin and became very involved in St. Cecilia's Catholic Church, where Bill led the funding drive and oversaw the construction of a new church in the mid 1980s.

Bill and Pat have three sons, Michael, Matt, and Charlie. Bill is a longtime financial supporter and advisor to COTS.

Interest in Volunteering and Charity

My volunteering started in our church. It started because my wife Pat was a very strong influence on me. She has always been the wind beneath my wings in terms of keeping me on the straight and narrow and doing the right thing. Pat would just say that one thing or another needs to be done down here at the church. And she would just look at me. I would say, "OK, I'll go down..."

What I remember from my upbringing is that we are here to help people who have less than we do. And Pat was very much the same way. She was a farmer's daughter from Nebraska. We never lived high off the hog, but we always gave.

Personal Philosophy

In *Walden*, Henry David Thoreau says "I have gone into the woods deliberately to live and not to find that when it came time to die that I hadn't lived." I read that as a junior in college and I said, "Man, that's what you've got to do. You have to live deliberately." That's probably been one of the most influential quotes of my life.

I also believe you have to give back, which is just a secular way of saying what is in the Bible. Read the gospels, you don't need to know anything more than that. I'm not going to create a new philosophy. I try really hard, and I don't always succeed. I fail many, many times, unfortunately. But I try really hard to follow those teachings.

Thoughts on Giving

When I was young I was taught that you read the gospel and you don't ignore it; you listen to it. My mother was big on telling us that it doesn't do you any good to hear this, that, or the other thing on a Sunday morning and just go off the rest of the week and be a Sunday Catholic (or Christian or Jew or whatever).

I was raised not to hoard stuff. You only need so much money to live on, feed your family, clothe them, put a roof over their heads, give them an education. You don't need any more money than that, really. So share it. When I was growing up, my family looked down on people that had flashy cars or extravagant lifestyles.

I remember hearing it is better to give than to receive. When I was 10, I thought that was dumb. But it's true! My son, Matt, used to go out and buy presents and invariably he'd come in the day before Christmas or your birthday and start giving you all these hints. "Don't you want to know what I got you? It's such a great thing!" The excitement of that was infinitely more than the excitement of him getting anything. I bet most people feel that way. I think most people feel good when they give. Giving is the embodiment of love.

Thoughts on the Work of COTS

I was raised on the idea that you have to be accountable. Why would you bring kids into the world if you weren't prepared to take care of them? I had some rough times in business in 1982, and just did whatever it took to pay my mortgage and feed my family. I still have strong feelings about this, but they've mellowed a bit. My wife has pointed out that not everyone is as disciplined and motivated as I am.

So I have asked, "Who are all these homeless people?" I didn't understand who they were, but I realized that many of them were people who should be taken care of, and weren't because of changes in the political situation.

The poor will always be with us. You have just got to make damn sure that, as I've said a number of times, that it's not the same people year after year. There will always be poor, but you want to move them up and out. And there are some people that simply aren't capable of handling things. And that's something that I had to open my heart to find out and COTS helped me do that. Brian Hoover from the Salvation Army helped me do that, too.

How COTS Fits his Philosophy

Christ was always taking care of the poor, or taking care of the lepers, and prostitutes. He had more feeling for those people who were down and out than he did for the Pharisees and the hot-shots of the day. An awful lot of what He says is about caring and love for people.

I say this often, and I have been saying this now for over 25 years, ever since I got over my "they can take care of themselves" attitude: The creatures of God deserve more than "they can take care of themselves." In fact, that's not true at all. It's our job to take care of each other.

The Meaning of Service

I think that God gives each of us different talents and skills, and He expects us to use them to provide for our families and our livelihoods. But he also expects if we are successful at doing that, we should use those same talents, skills and abilities to help others. Many people have a hard time just keeping their families going, and God bless 'em.

We've been successful at creating more than what we personally need. I've often said at my church when they needed my skills in particular, that it was my job. That's one of the reasons I am here, to do that job. I believe God would be very disappointed in me if I don't.

Christ changed the world by saying there are things that are more important than what meets the eye. I'm not saying you have to be a churchgoer or a Bible reader. There are people who will secularize it and that's fine. But to me, service and giving are not necessarily human nature. Human nature is many things, including greed. Some may think it's a part of human nature, because even when you give to people who are total strangers, it makes you feel good. But I would just say in my case that it's what God wants me to do.

III. THINKING OF THE CHILDREN

Nothing you do for children is ever wasted.
    —Garrison Keillor

There are only two lasting bequests we can hope to give our children. One is roots; the other, wings.
    —Hodding Carter

When I approach a child, he inspires in me two sentiments; tenderness for what he is, and respect for what he may become.
    —Louis Pasteur

If we don't stand up for children, then we don't stand for much.
    —Marion Wright Edelman

All children deserve nourishment, shelter, safety, and love. Homeless kids, like other children, experience life in an elemental way; they feel deeply, and they respond well to kindness.

Many volunteers find that working with homeless children teaches them a great deal, and affords them a richer perspective not only on homelessness, but on themselves and on humanity in general.

They also observe that homeless parents want desperately to provide well for their children.

Daymon Doss

"I was at COTS to learn as much as to give."

Background

Daymon Doss has volunteered at the COTS Center for Homeless Children and Their Families and at the Kitchen. He is trained as a Registered Nurse and respiratory therapist, and is the CEO of the Petaluma Health Care District.

Early Family Influence

My mother and father were both schoolteachers, born in the southern plains state of Oklahoma. They moved out to California in the late 1950s to teach school. I remember my father being very easygoing with seniors and older people, very affable with everyone. He always had two or three older persons whom he did things for. In my life, there was always a message through the family or through the church that you should be giving something, or doing something for others.

Involvement with COTS

I enjoyed volunteering at COTS because I felt like I was contributing something of myself. But in my role on the Board of Directors, if I had to do it over again, I would bring more of Daymon and less of "someone from the hospital." I always felt obligated to act in a certain way because I was a senior manager at the hospital. Homelessness includes a lot of healthcare issues, so there were times that I responded to proposals very cautiously: "Perhaps we can do that; maybe we can do this."

I think every Board has pure community members and also institutional members. Some people have to represent an institutional entity as much as they represent themselves. I was in that situation. And while that was not onerous, it would have been even more enjoyable to just represent myself.

I used to go to COTS on certain Sundays, rotating with other volunteers. At that time, in order to keep the shelter open on Sundays and control costs, volunteers were in charge sometimes. So I would come in on Saturday evening, and spend the night. I was there to make sure everything was secure and to be there in case there was any emergency, and also to be there in the morning to oversee breakfast and make sure everybody got up on time. There were certain times that people were supposed to get up and around, even if it was Sunday!

So the residents got up, made their breakfast, and some of the kids watched TV. If the weather was nice and they could play outside, I'd often go outside too and play some basketball, or kickball, or stand around and watch. I tried to be there for those who needed me, but not be obtrusive. This was their home; I didn't want to seem like a security guard or somebody with that attitude of "I'm here to keep you in line."

I was curious about the people, their motivations, and what was happening to them. How did they get there? But as a nurse, I respect privacy, so I never asked about anything. I just observed it and picked a lot up by watching.

I saw how parents interacted with each other and their children. I would watch them as they put their kids down on Saturday night, as they went to bed themselves, as they got up the next morning, and then at breakfast. I got to see how they treated one another, how they treated their children, and how they handled group living. You have to be pretty skilled to do group living; it can be tense, but I saw them deal with it incredibly well for the most part.

On occasion, usually during the holiday season, I would integrate my family a bit with what I was doing at COTS. We would all go over and cook a breakfast, so the clients wouldn't have to do that particular chore on that day.

Many Different Stories, Different Outcomes

Volunteering at COTS at the original resident center was a great experience for me. One time my wife Sally and I stepped in on behalf of a young couple and their child. They could not get an apartment. They had old PG&E debt, telephone debt, and utilities debt, so no one would rent to them. So Sally and I paid off their debt, and they left COTS and moved into an apartment in Santa Rosa.

Subsequently I learned from a helping agency that this young man was actually scamming a lot of people. But that really didn't bother us too much, because we felt that we had done what we did for the right reasons. Sally and I, when we were young, had often had very little money and had been in debt, and it would have been nice to have somebody take the pressure off. So we had been hoping that with some pressure off, the couple's relationship might improve and they would see some hope. That didn't happen. But it was a good experience for Sally and me; we saw that you can't get too attached to outcomes. It won't always be a storybook ending.

I heard some wonderful stories when I was on the COTS Board, but also stories in which people, even when you give them support for a period of time, are still unable to successfully make a transition.

COTS and Spiritual Practice

I could have been some place other than COTS on those Sunday mornings, but I have always been in search and in need of a spiritual structure. COTS provided that.

I don't have illusions about my actions or how long-lasting their effects will be. But they are connected to the Spirit of God. That's the key for me, and what I've learned is that you must practice. You're probably not going to spontaneously attain a high spiritual state by just walking down the street. It's possible, it could happen, it may have happened to many people. But my reality is that I have to practice.

For example, I need to practice using my intuition, about when to act and when not to act, about how to acknowledge someone, about how to encourage somebody, about when it's the right time to give support and the right time not to offer support, about when it's time to be quiet.

What Daymon Learned at COTS

I learned how deeply some of the residents' frustrations went. At times they blew me away. The children blew me away the most, because their lives were so different from how my childhood had been. As a child, I always had food, shelter, warmth, love, and support from lots of people. The isolation that some of the homeless children experienced was terrible.

Or when you've got a couple living in a car with two kids in the back seat, it's pretty amazing to see how they function. They are a family unit and that's their home, their shelter on wheels.

I was at COTS to learn as much as to give. I like learning. I was just soaking it up.

And there is something in there that tells you, "You should do this." The Holy Ghost, the Spirit of God is what moves me. That is what I have available to me. God does not reveal himself to me nor does Christ. So I don't see them directly, but I feel their Spirit.

Advice for Others on Service

Service needs to touch you. There's something that happens, I don't exactly know what it is but there's a feeling that happens when you've given something of yourself, of your true self, to someone else. Even if it's in a very small way, a little bit of time. And it keeps you going, it energizes you, it makes everything worthwhile. Rarely is it money, but it could be money.

You can be of service very simply just by smiling at a person at the right time, or opening a door for someone. I get a lot of satisfaction from that because I was raised in a place where being polite was very important. I am amazed at how much I say "Yes sir," "Yes, ma'am." I'm amazed especially at old folks, how much they just love that. You hold the door for someone and they'll say "Thanks." I'll say, "My pleasure." And it brings a smile. Just being nice to people is so meaningful.

Daymon's Hopes for His Own Children's Involvement

I would hope that my children have seen that Sally and I like to serve and we have found it of value. I hope that, as they grow, they will see service as a big part of their lives, not as something you do begrudgingly, but something you do almost automatically, with joy. Service energizes itself like one of those perpetual motion machines: the more you do it the better it feels and it becomes its own driver. There are an unlimited number of ways to be of service. If you have the resources, you have the responsibility.

Giving Yourself Away

"You're really going to get more out of service than you give." I used to hear that and think "Oh, ok." But it's really true. You really are going to get more out of it than you give.

It's hard to find what stirs your soul, but again, I think it takes practice. You've got to practice, whether it's sports or some intellectual exercise—or service. You need to practice giving of yourself, giving of your resources. It requires time and effort.

There are those, I'm sure, to whom it comes naturally, but for me I need to practice it. Eventually, I hope, it will become all-consuming—every breath, every act. I hope that, some day, I can give myself away completely. I'm going to go away some day anyway, so I might as well go away as I'm giving myself away.

Sherry Fink

"When you see how great the kids are that you're working with, it makes you love being there."

Background

Sherry Fink grew up in Shaker Heights, a suburb of Cleveland, Ohio. She earned an AA degree at the University of Toledo in computer programming in the late 1960s. She later returned there to complete a degree in Math, and then headed west to California. She is a teacher at Casa Grande High School in Petaluma.

Key Influences

My parents were pretty well off. They were always very generous, giving their time for volunteer work. My mom did that a lot, because in those days the moms didn't work. She volunteered in the hospital, and she was in quilting groups. She also used to transcribe things for the blind with Braille. My dad helped out for years at St. Malachay's church in Cleveland, serving dinner on Monday nights in the soup kitchen there. He and a bunch of his friends would go do that together.

Homelessness

I was in a semi-homeless situation when I was in my twenties. I wasn't living in the street, but I had just split up in a marriage and didn't have anywhere to go. I had a panel truck, and I used to sleep in the back of that. I had a bed back there, and I used to sleep in it and park the truck in my friends' driveway. If it got really cold, my friends had a basement—it was just a little crawl space, but I would climb in and sleep in there.

I never felt like I was desperate, because I had friends that would let me park in their driveway or sleep in their basement. So I felt fortunate.

After about six months, I saved enough money to share a house with someone by selling bagels at the flea market. We also walked up and down Fourth Street in San Rafael, and went to certain locations where there were shops, and we established a business that way. I didn't really think about it at the time as being anything that unusual; it was probably in the late '70's.

How Sherry Got Involved with Petaluma's Homeless

I wouldn't say that my time being homeless is what got me involved with the homeless. It more had to do with a guy that I met in town. I think I met him in the library because he hung out there a lot. We got to be good friends.

He didn't tell me that he was homeless. I would ask him if he needed a ride home, and he would say, "Well, just drop me off at the library; I'm meeting some friends there." Finally, as we got to be closer friends and he opened up more, he told me that where he slept was in the bushes on the side of the highway.

I went down there with him once or twice. There were sleeping bags and books, and there were other people sleeping around there; it was almost like a little community.

Around that same time, I began to realize that, as a teacher, I had a hundred and fifty students in my own classes and access to two thousand more students, and we could do something to blend the school and community and help people. So I said, "I want to do a club that's gonna help the homeless." And that's when I started the Helping Hands Club, in the year 2000. (At first we just called it "Help the Homeless" until the kids thought of a better name.)

When I first started it, I really didn't think it was going to grow in popularity and support like it has. Now kids in school leadership are involved, and a lot of classes that need community service hours will come and join the activities that our club does. We do the basic things like canned food drives and a warm clothing drive. At Christmas time we have a toy drive and then we go to COTS and some of the kids wrap the presents.

We have kids who work regularly at the family shelter, and some who work at the soup kitchen. They volunteer for certain days of the week, and they go in groups of two. At the family shelter, they tutor the kids or play with them. We also do group functions, like bringing Valentines to the kids.

The club meets every Wednesday at lunch for about 45 minutes. So this year we spent a couple of those Wednesdays designing Valentine's cards. The kids brought in material like doilies and different colored construction papers and sparkles and all kinds of art. And we made the cards and then we bought some candy, and then took the candy and cards over to the kids at the shelter. Then we spent a couple of hours with the kids while they opened their cards. They were really grateful, and such cute kids.

A lot of the Helping Hands Club's success has to do with kids that other kids look up to, like Amy and Leah, kids with big hearts who'll pull other kids in with them. Then other kids aren't afraid to say, "Yeah, I'm in the Helping Hands Club."

What Sherry Gets from this Service

I always look forward to the club meetings. I have a real sense of pride in the club—not only that it was kind of my creation—but that the kids accepted it, and they flocked towards it, without me pushing that much. It has fulfilled needs for different people in different ways. It's become a "cool" thing. It makes you feel good when you start something like that and people say, "Good for you, that's a great thing that you guys did."

A Letter from COTS

There was a letter that we got. Actually it was directed to one of our club members, Jesse. We had just gotten done with our toy drive; it was right after the holidays. The kids had gathered the toys and gone to stores to ask for donations—some even just bought new presents or found almost-new presents at home—and they took them and they wrapped them and gave them to some of the families in the shelter. And then we got a letter from a lady who said, "A year ago today I never thought I would be in this situation. I was married, we had good income, and I had a nice house and a nice family."

With the changing economy, her marriage fell apart, she ended up getting a divorce, she lost her job and didn't have the income of her ex-husband, and all of a sudden found herself with no home for herself or her children. She turned to COTS and they placed her in the family shelter. And she had so much appreciation for the kids at Casa Grande, who had given of themselves over the holidays to help people like her. It was such a touching letter. As Jesse was reading it aloud, we were just sitting there with our jaws open. Some of us were crying and had goosebumps. After hearing that letter, everyone said, "That's why we're here."

And this was just one person that wrote to us. There are probably a lot of people who don't write to us, who feel that way but don't put it in words and write a letter, but that probably are just as appreciative. And a lot of other people also find themselves in a situation that they never thought they'd be in a year ago, or a few years ago. So it makes you realize it can happen to anybody. And I think a lot of the kids *do* realize that; as they get to know the kids and the families, they see that they're just like us.

Philosophy

I believe that when people help other people, good things come back to them. I'm not sure if that's why I do it, or if it's just that it has put me in touch with a great group of kids. I love working with the kids. I love seeing them outside of school. I love when I'm driving down the street and kids honk and wave. I can't even imagine any other job that I would feel this strongly about. So this is an opportunity to work with kids outside of the classroom environment, and get to know them and become friends with them.

What COTS Means to Sherry

COTS is a wonderful organization that's really meeting the needs of a large part of the population in Petaluma. I'm honored to be part of it. Everyone knows the name of COTS in Petaluma; it's a well-known name. But I don't think there are very many people that know all the things that COTS does. I never realized how large it was until I got involved, and got to know people there. I never even knew about the Opportunity Center, or the swim center being turned into the family shelter. I had lived here in Petaluma for twenty years and never knew, until I started this club.

Advice for Others on Service

I would encourage anybody who wants to get involved with kids, to bring out the best qualities in kids, and get to know them. When you see how great the kids are that you're working with, it makes you love being there.

Carrie Hess

"Luckily, I got to see these kids as they slept . . ."

Background

Carrie Hess has volunteered at the COTS Center for Homeless Children and Their Families and has held various COTS positions working with children and parents. She currently directs the Kids First program, which she developed.

Parental Inspiration

We moved around quite a bit when I was young, but we were a relatively solid family. My parents had a lot of integrity, and expected people to tell the truth and to be compassionate. I thought, growing up, that I was getting away with a lot of stuff that my parents didn't know about. But when we finally started talking about it, I was surprised to find out that they knew about a lot of the things I did, but they trusted me enough to figure that I would pay the price for my bad choices, and learn from my good choices. They let me go as far as I needed to, in hope that I'd come out of it okay. I think that's a big leap of faith for parents to make: I don't know that I can do that with my kids. There's so much out there that can get in the way of my kids building the life they want for themselves.

Human Connection as Service: A Lesson Learned Young

When I was in elementary school in southern California, the school had one section for mainstream students, and another section for children with mental, physical and developmental disabilities. Part of the curriculum was for both types of students to participate in programs together so we would integrate. I made a connection with kids I hadn't really understood before, whom I had shied away from because they were so different. I soon had some very strong connections with those kids and I found that just connecting however you could—in a non-verbal way, in kindness and respect—mattered so much to them and to me. That made a huge impression on me.

A Life Change, A Call to Service

After college I worked in Fortune 500 companies doing marketing and advertising. Those jobs paid well and were fun but were not all that inspiring. Eventually I got married and moved to Europe. We were supposed to be over there for two years, but two years turned into ten. I was in Zurich for five years and then London for five years. I worked for a while, then had a baby and stopped working to stay home full time. Unlike in the U.S., in Switzerland the whole system is set up to support mothers raising their children.

When I returned to the States in 1998, I was a single mom with two young daughters. I was searching for something that would feel meaningful. Previously I had given money to agencies and to people in the subways and people who came to the door—I didn't buy what they were selling, but I donated to them. It didn't feel like enough. I wanted to do more but didn't know what else to do. I didn't feel like I was reaching out to people effectively just by handing them some money. It was too easy, and it wasn't very meaningful to me, and I didn't know how meaningful it was to the other people either.

Working with COTS

Not long after I returned from Europe I got a holiday mailing from COTS. My older daughter and I were trying to figure out something special to do together at Christmas time. So we called the family center, and talked to the Haven director. We made some muffins and other foods for the Haven and volunteered.

My daughter and I had expectations of what volunteering at COTS would be like. I believe my daughter thought she'd be holding babies and comforting people, and I kind of thought the same thing. But we got there during a period in Haven when they had a lot of big boys. My daughter was completely intimidated by them: she couldn't speak, she wouldn't sit down; she was just completely taken aback by these boys. But then we went outside to play. We spent three hours with those boys, playing tag and running around, and we had just the greatest time. When we were driving home that first time she said to me, "I can't believe it, Mom, those kids are just like me!" That was a big learning experience for her to have in such a short time; she was really happy and amazed. So was I.

One thing that is personally satisfying for me is being a team player at COTS and having relationships with coworkers. We work together to make a difference and we support one another. That makes me love what I do every day; it makes it a pleasure to come in and to be here.

The work requires a lot of energy. In the Haven it was very difficult at first, because I really didn't have a background in child care; I had been raising my own two children, but as far as children in crisis, I didn't have experience in that. So it was a sink-or-swim situation. My first week I had bruises up and down my legs, One child spat in my face; kids had called me all sorts of names that were very creative and shocking. But luckily I got to see these kids as they slept, and hold them when they woke up, and I understood that there was something in them that they needed to release. I understood that being somebody who was safe for them, someone who they could trust with their hurt and anger, was a positive thing; and that they were able to act in these ways because they trusted me. So I needed to strengthen

my boundaries and work with them on understanding that anger is something we all feel; it's how we express it that's important.

I saw remarkable changes in some of the children, and I found it really
hard to let go when it was time for them to leave. We had some children
that came to us in terrible distress, who turned around to a point where they
could feel accepted and successful. To see a child come in not speaking, not
laughing, not crying, not showing any emotion, and within three weeks to
see them riding a bike and laughing out loud, and crying when somebody
threw them down on the ground, and crawling into your lap and talking to
you, was amazing. I was getting back much more than I was putting out.
That feeling of having a child trust and rely on you, and being able to give
them something that they needed when they needed it—*that* was what I'd
been searching for.

The Influence of Children

I've always had a real connection with children. I knew when I was a
young teenager that I wanted to have kids, and I wanted to be a mother, and
I wanted to nurture. That was a really strong desire for me, to nurture other
people. I wanted to know that I was doing something other than focusing
on just myself. And when I had kids that really became clear: my life was no
longer just about me; it was about kids and about the world, and about what
kind of world my children would inherit when they were older. I love
knowing that I'm passing on something important to my kids, so that they
too are givers.

Working with *Kids First*

I'm currently the *Kids First* program manager. I teach the twelve-week
Kids First class, for parents and kids. We provide parenting education for the
adults, and we build a developmentally appropriate curriculum for the
children. We work with kids ages zero to seventeen; we nurture them and
make sure the younger kids are hitting their developmental milestones, and

that the school-age kids have a voice and understand the importance of being proactive in their own lives.

When you work with the kids, you see all the struggles they're having and you think, "Oh, I wish these parents would just do what they have to do to soothe their kids!" But in working with the parents, I realize that they also didn't have their needs met as children. Some parents spend their lives screaming at their kids because that's all they know how to do. Just about every person in their life who was supposed to love and protect them has let them down. So they're trying to parent their children without a good model of what that looks like. At the same time they're trying to find some way to get an income so that they can afford a place to live. Many of them are single parents, mostly single moms.

So we ask a lot of them. We ask them to go back to school and back to work; we ask them to treat their kids well and find transportation if they don't have it. And they put their heads down and lean into it and do the best they can. When I started, I didn't realize how tough it is, how much of a burden it is for them. But they want to do right by their children.

It's important to try to help them feel empowered insofar as we can, because we have a lot of rules. They're adults, but we're telling them they have to do this chore, and they have to have their kids in bed by this time, and this is the time that they have to eat, and this is the food they have to choose from. It sometimes makes them feel like children themselves. So, the more we're able to be supportive and respectful, then the more effectively we can model what healthy relationships look like, and what trust can feel like, and what good relationships with kids might be like.

We give kids a chance to speak their mind and we let them know that it's okay to feel all the emotions that they feel. We explain that the important thing is how they express those feelings, and that we all struggle with that sometimes. We tell the parents that too, and hopefully they model self-control for their kids. We help parents get their own needs met so they can meet the needs of their children. When parents do better their kids do better and the family is strengthened. That's the goal.

Transitional Housing

We have a transitional housing program, with eleven houses in Roh- nert Park and Petaluma, with two or three or sometimes four families living in each house. It's a very challenging way for them to live. Living with your own family or friends is hard enough, but living with strangers who all have their own idea about who should do what, what a clean house looks like, what good parenting looks like, and then being judged by those people, and having them talk behind your back, is very stressful. It's hard to be making all your mistakes in a very public way.

We visit the families in these homes. We mediate conflicts and try to help them recognize that being supportive of one another is much more productive than tearing each other down. We support them in developing the skills they need to reach their potential as adults and as families, to build the kinds of lives they really want.

Advice for Others on Service

What inspires any one person to service is very personal. You have to look at your strengths and your desires, and look into your heart to discover what you have to give that's most meaningful, for you and for others. If something comes up, an opportunity for service that resonates for you, go for it! Experience it! If you see a number on a flyer and it intrigues you, call it. It may not be perfect for you forever, but it may be what you're looking for at the time. Every step you take, even if it's difficult, will propel you forward toward what you're really looking for.

The Upward Spiral

I've had a lot of positive experiences with clients who have come through extremely difficult times, and have come out the other side, and are now looking at how they can give back. One client who had a really tough time said she recognizes that she now has the opportunity to help other people come through, because she's seen that it's possible. She said, "I want to work for COTS or a place like COTS, because COTS has made all the difference for me."

When we offer ourselves out in the world, or in our immediate sur-roundings, it creates a domino effect. People are touched by it and they realize that they have something to give too. You multiply it by all the folks we work with and all their children who will have a better life, and I think it's going to make a difference in the world. A spiral doesn't always have to be a downward spiral; it can raise people up and contribute to the goodness, the compassion, and the love in the world.

Diane Landman

"Where there's life, there's hope."

Background

Diane Landman grew up in San Francisco, California in a traditional 1950s "Leave it to Beaver"-type neighborhood. She married her high school sweetheart, Ed, and moved to Petaluma in 1972. They have two sons, two daughters-in-law, one granddaughter and one grandson. Diane began volunteering for COTS after her children were grown, and then gradually assumed various staff positions. After 15 years of service at COTS, she retired in October 2007 from her position as Director of COTS' Housing and Family Services program.

How Her Background Influenced Her Interest in Others

My parents taught me at an early age the customary axiom "Do unto others as you would have others do unto you." When I turned six, my grandmother came to live with us. She would read from the Bible and she believed in the Ten Commandments. She taught me the importance of respect. If she saw something that she didn't like me doing, she would never say, "You shouldn't have done that." Instead, she would ask me, "How do you think the other person feels?"

I was always taught to care about other people -- to value everybody. I remember when, as a child, I learned how hurtful people could be. We were a middle class neighborhood in San Francisco, and one year we were having the annual 4th of July party. Everyone was invited to the gathering except for one family who lived up the street. The reason was that they rented their house, instead of owning it.

I was nine or ten at the time, and I thought "Why can't they come?" These people were really nice, but they were judged by what they had, not by who they were. That gave me a new outlook on prejudice, to learn that my own neighbors would behave this way. Why would that friend be different from another friend across the street just because they rented their house?

How Diane Discovered COTS

I had a very challenging year after my mother passed away suddenly. At the same time my current place of employment went through reorganization. It was time to for me stop and make some changes. Then I read an article by John Records in the *Argus Courier* and I was very impressed by it. And at the time, my daughter, Stacy, was saying she wanted to do more community service and she loved working with kids.

Back then, it was actually hard to find COTS, it wasn't well-known, so I decided to accompany my daughter on her first trip to volunteer there. When we first came to the shelter, we immediately noticed the warm, welcoming feeling, and before I knew it she was working with kids and I was helping out in the office!

I liked being at COTS and knew there was something special about it. I liked being around all of these great people who wear their hearts on their sleeves, these caring, wonderful people.

Coping with Challenges

I'm the type of person who sees hope. When there's life, there's hope.

At the end of the day, no matter what happens, I always reflect on the positive moments of the day. And maybe if this or that objective didn't get accomplished, we were at least able to provide this service or that service for a child—we were able to get them shoes, or whatever was needed to make them know we care about them. When I hear kids calling COTS "home," then I know we have really made a difference and that they see this place as being special, a place where they can *be* kids, a safe place.

Staff come and go, but everyone has left what I call a "heart print" on the agency. I enjoy having all of the pictures around of everyone who has had a part in COTS and really cared.

There are some days when there is a lot of sadness in this work, but there are bright days as well. I know that I can't please every client every time and I can't please every staff person every time. And I'm OK with that.

Why Diane Stays Connected to COTS

I believe in the work. When I first get the families into the Family Center, that very first night when they arrive, they're at a very tough point in their lives. Once they come into COTS, they get comfortable with the way we provide services for them. Just smiling at them and giving them a supportive look, just something as easy as that is what inspires me.

I also love it when I see the kids smile. When someone can look you in the eye for the first time with their growing pride and you can have a conversation with them, it feels good to do this work.

My main reason for staying is the children and the families. We can make a difference. What has been really nice with the growth of our services is that you can see the people along the whole path as they come through the family center, and then the housing program, and then more and more independence. It's very rewarding when you really see the families are in a better place.

One Family's Story

The saying "it takes a village" enters into our work on a daily basis. A mom pregnant with her second child, a dad, and their little two-year-old son arrived at the Family Center. With a baby on its way, this family wanted to get settled into a safe and nurturing place as soon as possible. A housing option had fallen through for this family and they ended up at COTS. The baby arrived prematurely. The doctors warned he had a hernia that would eventually require surgery. The family came back to the family shelter with the baby. This family was already in crisis and trying to do the best they could do to be good parents. The family struggled to tend to their new baby. Any time the baby coughed, sneezed, or burped his intestines would burst into his scrotum. Then his surgery was delayed because it was not clearly defined as an emergency. And it would take three or four additional weeks for all the paperwork to go through. In the meantime the baby cried.

John Records was visiting the family shelter and when he heard about this family, he felt they were in an unacceptable situation. He phoned a friend of COTS, a longtime COTS supporter. This person knew how to work his way through the medical system to find help for this little baby and family. Once this person brought this situation to the attention of those that could make the surgery happen, they were very helpful. This friend of COTS later said, "When you have an opportunity to assist and when you have another opportunity later to meet the parents and hold the baby, this is why we do this work."

An update: the family left the family shelter and moved to Idaho where the dad found work and reunited with his family there. I heard from the family last year that they have housing, and if they are out our way they will stop by. They remember COTS fondly, and were thankful COTS was here when they needed help. They added that we won't recognize the baby as he is now a healthy, happy, and active two-year-old boy.

Many families who have been here come back some time later when they are doing better, and they say, "I want to volunteer." They come back because this was a good place for them and they want to give back. They remember. It's not like they leave COTS and forget about it. They care and they come back.

It's amazing when you can see everything come full cycle. But then there are the people that you know you do the best that you can for, and then we have to let them make their choices and we need to be OK with it and remember that even if they haven't completely succeeded, they got something from us. They received some warmth and shelter and their kids were nourished for a time. We know we did everything we could do.

Philosophy and Beliefs

I believe that people *can make positive changes in their lives*, and that everybody should have a chance—especially the children, who are in these situations through no fault of their own.

Once you start talking with people at the shelter, you find you can relate really easily. So, you have to believe in people, not be judgmental, and if there's a way to help them, I think we should do that.

COTS came into my life at a special time. I don't know why it happened but it has provided a kind of wholeness for me. It was a time when my kids were gone, they had moved out and gone to college, and COTS gave me a place to feel needed.

Thoughts for Others about Service and Giving

I would tell everybody that it's a good feeling to serve people. It's better to give than receive.

I tell people that I think you have to be in a balanced place yourself and you have to have definite boundaries, which are important, because of some of the experiences you will have. But there is always a need for service, and I think that if a person is giving and they can see it makes a difference, that's a great joy.

The amazing thing to me, really, is the resilience of people. I'm just very thankful to be able to do this work and I appreciate all the people that make it possible.

Amy Mastick

"If everyone lent a helping hand,
even more would be accomplished."

Background

When she was three, Amy Mastick moved to Petaluma from Marin County with her parents. She became involved in COTS through the Helping Hands Club at Casa Grande High School. She was a senior at Casa Grande at the time of her interview.

Since then, Amy has been studying Psychology at Sonoma State University and teaching children's dance classes at Suzanne's Dance School in Petaluma. She has done volunteer work with other Sonoma State University students, such as working at the Redwood Empire Food Bank and traveling to New Orleans to rebuild homes with Habitat for Humanity.

Role Model for Volunteering

My biggest role model was my mom. I was brought up knowing the importance of helping others. She used to help children who were less fortunate by buying and donating needed items; she did Christmas shopping for children in need, things like that. So, my mom was the one who originally inspired me.

I don't remember ever sitting down and being taught the importance of helping others. I remember just knowing it was the right thing to do. I learned by example.

Connecting to COTS

I was with the Helping Hands Club at Casa Grande High School when the club first started. Ms. Fink and another student started the club, and since I was in Ms. Fink's class, she told me I should sign up. I let her know that I was interested and began going to meetings. I later became President of the club.

Our club has mostly done warm clothing drives and toy drives. We have also focused on getting other students involved and increasing awareness. I did a lot of tutoring and playing with the kids at COTS when I was a sophomore. I went to the shelter every Friday for a few hours.

Making Time for Volunteering as a Teen

Other students might find different activities more fun, but I can't really think of anything that would be more worthwhile or productive than helping people out. Especially kids. I've always had an interest in kids, and I work at a preschool so I have a lot of experience working with kids.

Challenges While Volunteering with COTS

The most challenging thing was getting to know the families and kids really well, and then having them leave, because they're only there for a few months. I always wonder how they're doing after they go.

It's not at all depressing to be there volunteering. The kids understand what's going on, but they're still happy to be where they are. It isn't a depressing place with the playground, books, toys, and plenty of fun activities. The kids are having just as much fun as they would anywhere else. They're all friends. It's not sad to see people living there because it is such a positive atmosphere and a great place to be.

Philosophy about Volunteering

I believe in helping others. Not everyone's as lucky as many students here are. People have things happen to them and get put in positions that they don't necessarily want to be in, and don't know how to get out of. I think I've been pretty lucky. All the people in the Helping Hands Club have been pretty lucky. So we're happy to help other people who do not have the opportunities we have been given.

What COTS Means to Amy

I would say COTS represents helping others and giving people a chance. A lot of people who work there are volunteers, or they work for low pay. It's a whole group of people who are similar to the Helping Hands Club, in that they want to help out and spread the luck. COTS and the Helping Hands Club are united in their goal to help others, which in turn makes us all happy and enriches all of our lives.

Advice for Others about Volunteering or Being Involved in Service

I would suggest that all people share some of their time with any organization that they are passionate about. A lot of people just assume that other people will volunteer, and there's really not as many people helping out as you would think. I think that volunteering serves a larger purpose than just hanging out with your friends after school or watching television does. Volunteering is a lot more meaningful and productive. If everyone lent a helping hand, even more would be accomplished in our community.

Beth Wissing-Healy

"However you do it, service really does help you stay connected with humanity, and also with people around the community that you might not know exist but who are in need of help."

Background

Beth Wissing-Healy served as a COTS board member, and has volunteered at the COTS Center for Homeless Children and Their Families and at the Kitchen. She is a Public Defender living in Petaluma.

Family Influence

My parents were always volunteering when I was growing up. It was just part of what we did, primarily with our church. We would cook food for the Catholic Worker, and so we'd be preparing meals, or clothing, or whatever needed to be done. We had so much. We were a middle-class family, and we never wanted for food or warm things or lots of love.

Volunteer History

I went to the University of Iowa. I took one semester off, working in the 1980s for the Democratic Party. Then I took my last semester off and I worked in Washington, DC for a legal service. I also worked for the League of Women Voters Education Fund, doing voter service, research, and writing. Then I decided on law school, and thought I needed to go someplace different. I'd never been to San Francisco, so I decided to go there, and then started working for the California Advocates for Nursing Reform and the National Sanctuary Defense Fund, raising money to support litigation for the sanctuary workers. I also worked at Saint Anthony's, at the soup kitchen, and then at a battered women's shelter.

Religious Upbringing

My faith has influenced my volunteering. The philosophy is that you can't live your life without giving back to other people. For some reason I've been blessed with so much, and that's part of why I think I need to give back by volunteering. It's one thing to read the Gospels which preach that you should feed the hungry and clothe people. But it's another thing to practice it. So I was strongly influenced by activists within the church who set a wonderful example of service.

Noticing Need All Around Us

There is poverty everywhere. I was doing door-to-door campaigning for a candidate while volunteering for the Democratic Party in Washington, DC. I would go into parts of the city where I had never been before, and knock at doors. Someone would open up, and there were at least ten people living in a home the size of a dining room. They had so little, and it was incredible to see that. You don't have to go very far, wherever you are, to see the need all around you and the disparity between the haves and have-nots. When I lived in Washington, I lived a few blocks from the gorgeous town houses of the wealthy, but also just a few blocks from crack addicts' houses and great poverty. I worked for a homeless shelter for women at that time. A group of people and I would drive around in a van one night a week with coffee and food, trying to talk to people and see if they needed anything. We tried occasionally to talk them into going to a shelter, if possible.

Especially in the winter, so many of the poor and homeless would congregate around the sidewalk grates seeking heat. I would often see them gather around the White House and the other office buildings. It was very eye-opening.

Working with COTS

When I moved to Petaluma after I got married, I wanted to continue some volunteer work. I was still going into San Francisco on Sundays to work at Saint Anthony's at the soup kitchen. But I wanted to do something locally. One day I saw in the paper that COTS was holding a meeting. I learned more about the organization, and that they needed help. It was great, because I had time, and it was a very welcoming group. So I started working at the family shelter with the kids. I would come and volunteer with the children, or just be there in the evenings to play with the kids while the parents were doing other things, like cleaning up or doing laundry.

I also worked as a mentor at Rent Right one summer, and I've been doing the hospital run with the food on Friday afternoons—that is, getting excess food at the hospital and bringing it to the Op center. And during the winter we do the meals through Saint James on Sundays.

Challenges and Growth at COTS

It can be very challenging, trying to connect with people and help them without feeling that I might be seen as this judgmental middle-class woman telling them how they should spend their time and money. I've learned that it's important to be interested in people. It's important not to be judgmental toward people, whether it's toward how they're acting or the lifestyle decisions they've made. Some folks are just very troubled or unhappy. This has given me more insight into my own growth, where I still have work to do around being understanding. I think any time you try to stretch yourself, and you talk to new people, you grow.

Service as Connection

You see people who have dedicated their entire lives working for peace and for the poor. And for some of us, it's not our path to serve at that level. Still, it's important to reach out and do something. Some people have a lot of money they can give, and some people have a lot of time. But however you do it, service really does help you stay connected with humanity, and also with people around the community that you might not know exist but who are in need of help. Do something you can feel good about, that is a service to people in need. You can dedicate your life to service even in seemingly small ways and stay connected to humanity.

Philosophy on Service

I feel that I need to be of service. I find that if I'm not, I feel empty or hollow inside.

I work every day with poor people in trouble. Though I really enjoy my work as a public defender, it's very stressful. I do the best I can, trying to get people through the criminal justice system, and trying to get them into a drug program or send them to health services. But it's more than something I'm doing for others; it's also something I do for myself.

Teaching Kids About Service

My daughter, when she was smaller, came to COTS with me and helped out. My kids both work for the Kitchen on Sundays, which makes us all happy. But life isn't just all about making yourself happy. You need to help others be happy, too. I want to teach my kids that.

Finding Hope and Joy Amid Adversity

One of the most amazing things about the family shelter at COTS is how joyful and hopeful it makes people. We see kids who are scared and don't have a place to live and may not know safety or a sense of love. But when they go to the family shelter they feel safe, which can lead to other positive feelings. Working here, I've seen that we can find happiness, joy, connection, and love amidst all kinds of pain. I think that's the glory of life. We all are going to experience pain, even if we're happy people and have family and friends. We will lose people we love, have problems with various areas of our lives, etc. There will always be pain, but it doesn't mean that there's no hope. COTS gives a lot of hope to people, and certainly hope for the children. Even if their parents are struggling very hard, they need to know that there are people out there who care about them, who will read them a book or give them a snack, give them a place to feel safe and loved.

Advice to Others on Service

My advice would be to just try it. I've never met a volunteer who thought service was a waste of time. What we gain from service, and what you give to someone else, is so rewarding.

IV. REWARDS OF SERVICE

The only ones among you who will be really happy are those who will have sought and found how to serve.
    —Albert Schweitzer

As you forget self in service to others, you will find that, without seeking it, your own cup of happiness will be full.
    —Paramahansa Yogananda

The rewards of service run wide and deep. Invariably, volunteers report that they "get back" more than they could have imagined. Some say they see themselves in a new light; others report that their lives have been infused with energy and warmth.

Paradoxically, you can't go into service with the *intention* of gaining something. Then again, you *can* do that, but you might get something different than you thought. In any case, there are always surprises.

Jim March

"I believe that by doing something, I can change whatever it is that's got me down."

Background

Jim March is a long-time friend and financial supporter to COTS. His unique volunteer activities with COTS have included building the awning area for the children's play center, and—every Friday for more than a year—going out for a few hours with Opportunity Center clients to plant and prune flowers and pick up garbage in the surrounding community.

Childhood

My Dad was a college professor. My Mom also went to college to be an English teacher. When they had kids, she stayed home to take care of us. They both come from the Midwest. I find that most people I meet from the Midwest have a strong tradition of being honest, hardworking, and caring. My parents raised me with a sense that you need to help other people. My dad always told me, "Don't judge someone by their name, or their parents, or their family. Judge people by what they do."

All four of my mother's grandparents came from Germany to settle in Wisconsin. It's not very long ago that my family was struggling. We needed help, we got help, and we succeeded. I have felt a close connection with recent immigrants, who may have had travesty or difficulty in their lives. I don't judge them as failures.

My parents were also very concerned about racial prejudice. I can remember standing in line with Mom and Dad in Pittsburgh, Pennsylvania, when I was nine years old. We were mailing letters asking the president to pass civil rights laws. My parents were insistent that everyone should have equal opportunity. Being young, I didn't understand what it all meant, but it got me to pay attention in school, to the way some people would prejudge others, or the way that I was prejudged. I became sensitive to prejudice.

I also remember how, when I was 8 years old, I would watch Tarzan movies on TV. Tarzan was a do-gooder. He wanted to help the animals. From my earliest days of being influenced by television, I was struck with this idea that if I don't do it, who will? Of course, my understanding of what that means has changed over the years.

Growing Up, Gaining Perspective

I was very fortunate to live in Europe for a year when I was sixteen. This was 1970-71. I was naïve at the time; I had been living a sheltered life in Orange County, California. How sheltered was I? Let me put it this way: my junior high school would not allow Tarzan in the library because Tarzan was not married to Jane and they had an illegitimate child together.

I lived for a year with a Belgian family that spoke no English. I went to a public school, where only two people spoke English. I was forced to learn another culture. I got an opportunity to see how another culture views America, and it was an eye-opener. I was surprised that most of the kids my age felt that the United States was doing terrible things. They would ask, "Why are there race riots? Why do the police have to beat black people? Why do they have to hit them over the head with those billy clubs and shoot those water cannons at them?" There were questions about the Vietnam War, about American economic interests around the world, and our grabbing for raw materials. There was a lot of criticism of the United States, as well as tremendous gratitude for our role in beating Hitler in World War II. So I came back home and started to look into things for myself. Much to my surprise, I found out that almost everything I had been told in Europe was true.

Another experience I remember was going to see the movie *Dr. Zhivago*. I was a sophomore in college, about 20 years old. I didn't give a hoot about the love story or the politics. There was a shot where we see a stream of displaced people in carts and horses. They had lost their homes and had to move for fear of being killed. I remember sobbing, and feeling the terrible pain of all of that suffering. I thought, "How could humans treat each other that way?"

Trying to Change the World

I worked for the things that I thought America stood for: the United Farm Workers helping immigrant labor, prison reform, and ending the Vietnam War. Feeling frustrated with the small impact I had on larger issues, I got involved with local politics. I didn't feel like I made a difference there either. I shrank my circle further. By age 26, I had graduated college and gotten married. At age 35, we had our first child. My circle shrank to the point that I was just taking care of my family. After 18 years of marriage and three children, my wife and I divorced. I had failed even in my smallest circle of responsibility.

I questioned myself: "What do I believe in? Why do I exist?" As I went through my divorce, I looked at my life and I realized that most of the things I was doing were for me. I was self-centered. At that point, I said, "How can I do good and not be self-centered?" I began to realize that I can't do good unless I know what "good" means to other people.

Taking Responsibility for the Consequences of Helping

Working with homeless folks, I'll ask, "What do you need? What do you want to do that would make your life fuller?" I also work with Habitat for Humanity. It's very easy to think that if I just give money, that I'm doing good. But I actually have to be more involved than that. There are many ways I can build homes for people that won't do them any good.

When I work for a non-profit, I make sure that it's not just icing, that we're actually delivering something that somebody needs. And that the results are actually produced. I always thought I knew what the world needed. Now I know that I don't know what the world needs. And, I'm here to help.

What does the world need? How do I find that out? Only through personal involvement. If I look at people who *really* do good, they are the ones who understand and are involved with the consequences of their actions and how their actions impact the people they're helping.

Protesting the Vietnam War, picketing for the United Farm Workers, and lobbying for prison reform were worthy efforts. But I was naïve about the complexity of those issues, and about other people's perspectives. I have learned that the world is not the way I imagine it is—particularly when I want to do good. I know that I *should* do good, but I wasn't taught *how* to do good.

To do good, I need to pay attention to what people need and take responsibility for the consequences of my involvement. Too many times I have thought that I was helping, but in the end, at best, the results were short-lived, and at worst, detrimental.

Changing People's Perceptions

What doesn't work is preaching. I'm done preaching. I am done telling people how they are wrong. Telling people "I am right and you are wrong" rarely changes a person's mind. I might tell them the way I think it should be, and if they don't agree, that's their choice. I'll tell people what I believe, but I don't tell people that they need to change. I give people options, ask them to make a decision, and hold them to the consequences, their part in the results.

Instead of changing people, I offer an alternative way of behaving to the people around me.

For example, when I'm taking care of the raised flower beds at the library, I pick up all the cigarette butts in front of the library. One fellow who was working with me said, "I'm not going to pick up any cigarette butts. I don't like to touch things that have been in other people's mouths." I said, "Yeah, you're right." Then I thought, "What the heck. If it doesn't kill me, it'll make me stronger." I pick up cigarette butts because I don't like the butts on the ground. Even while people are smoking, I will pick up cigarette butts around their feet. I don't tell them, "Stop throwing your cigarette butts on the ground." Instead, I pick up the butts. The smoker might think, "I wonder why that guy is picking up the butts?" Maybe he'll stop and think before he throws that butt down.

Another example is my commitment to pick up ten pieces of trash every day. When I walk around Petaluma, I see lots of litter. If I wanted to, I could spend my whole day picking up litter. But I won't do it. What I will do is pick up ten pieces of litter every day. Maybe, if someone sees me picking up litter, he will decide to pick up a few pieces, too. When I'm walking with people, I don't hesitate to bend over and pick up a piece of trash. Sometimes someone will ask me, "Why are you doing that? You can't pick up all the litter in Petaluma. There's too much." I answer, "Well, I don't like to see litter. If I don't pick it up, the litter stays. If I pick it up, it's gone."

Now, one might argue that picking up other people's litter only encourages people to continue to litter, but that has not been my experience. There is a road on the way from the COTS dining room to the library where people threw litter every day. Every week I walked by the litter with the folks from COTS on the way to the library garden, where we were growing flowers. One week, I couldn't stand it anymore. I reached down as I was walking and picked up a few pieces of trash. The folks that were with me started picking up trash, too. By about the third week, we had picked up all the trash along that stretch of half of a block. After that, we only picked up a few pieces of litter a week. It's as if, because it was clean, people didn't throw trash there anymore.

My goal is to keep Petaluma clean, but I'm not preaching about it. I'm just going out every day and picking up trash.

My Responsibility

I believe it's my responsibility to use everything I've been given to the best of my ability. I feel a sense of fulfillment when I go beyond what I thought I could do. That's the epitome of human accomplishment, and I don't care what level I'm at, but if I'm going beyond what I thought I could do, that's my tribute to being a human being.

Going beyond what I thought I could do brings up a wellspring of wonderment, enjoyment, and love. That's what drives me. I'll just use the example of the "unexpected flowers" program at the library. When we finish for the day, I say, "Turn around and look at what we did." I allow a moment for us to experience what we've accomplished by picking up trash and tending flowers. I ask, "How do you think people will feel when they walk into the library, now? Is the library more inviting? Does it feel like a friendlier place? Like somebody cares?" And that's our tribute to humanity, our own and all the people who experience what we've done.

It's taken me a long time to learn the discipline of putting aside what I want for what another person needs. When I had kids, I learned about giving myself up to my children. I have expanded that to giving myself up for my community. I continue to ask myself, "What does my community need? What does my country need? What does humanity need?"

Awe

I am an eternal optimist. I don't stay down or depressed for very long. I believe that by doing something, I can change whatever it is that's got me down.

I've been curious all my life. I live very much in awe. I feel like I'm always a ten-year-old. When I look at a flower, I say, "My God, that's so beautiful." I'm completely awestruck by it.

When I travel, my wife loves to listen to me because all my senses go on high alert. She enjoys the way I see the world. We went to Paris last summer and I took my youngest daughter out on walks. I would tell her what I was paying attention to. I remember telling her, "Let's count how many different kinds of street lamps we find on our walk home." And we did. We were hard pressed to find two that were alike. Just that perspective made walking home a completely different experience.

When I walk with my kids, I'll stop and say, "Look at this tree. This leaf is about to come out. Let's check tomorrow to see if it comes out." It's a way of being present. It's a way of being alive.

Being in awe is one of the reasons I paint. Painting is a way of looking at something. I can look at the same thing a thousand times but when I paint it I see it differently. I pay attention to details that I never thought about before. Human beings are capable of being far more aware than we usually are. I get little glimpses of that when I listen to music or I look at a painting. What if I could see the world the way that Van Gogh painted? I *can* do that, if I pay attention. The world *is* like a Van Gogh painting.

I know I must understand as much as I can, but I also know that I will never understand everything. To be in awe, I have to let go of thinking that I can understand everything. Surrendering to being humble lets me experience awe.

Spiritual Philosophy

My parents were brought up with some formal religion, but they chose not to expose me to it. But without religious dogma, I've become much more religious than my parents are. I have come to believe that God exists, though I also know that God is something I will never understand, and is misunderstood by most religions. My brain has a limited capacity to understand things. God is more complex than I can understand, though I do experience perspectives, or facets, of God. I am one of those facets.

I want to see the human species move to a new level, a new level of understanding and capability. Even as we begin to understand how the human brain works, it is so unbelievably more complex and powerful than we ever imagined. I believe that the next step for the human species is for us to continue to become more cooperative, working together to achieve things beyond what we ever thought we could achieve.

Thoughts on Service

One of the greatest benefits of working with homeless people is being reminded that there are many different ways of living. And to think that I know the right way to live is pretty small-minded.

I feel most capable, human, and empowered when I help someone else. I will never satisfy my wants, so I choose to help others satisfy their needs. If I leave this world a better place than I found it, I will die a happy man.

Angie Sanchez

"You always receive by giving;
it's the great circle of life."

Background

Angie Sanchez was on the COTS Board of Directors and a volunteer in the COTS kitchen. Angie now resides in Costa Rica, but she keeps in touch.

Early Family Influence

My interest in volunteering started with my mother. When I was growing up in Southern California, she used to volunteer in schools, particularly school clean-up projects. When I was a child, we volunteered cleaning up parks in the community and helped out with various other clean-up projects. My father also influenced me. He worked a bit with the homeless, and introduced me to that world. When I was seven or eight, he invited a homeless couple to spend the holidays with us.

Volunteer History

When I came to Marin County, I volunteered teaching English as a Second Language and helped with the Bookmobile, taking library books out to the ranches. I also did some volunteer work in Petaluma with the Hispanic Cultural Development Corporation. They put on events that help the community and raise money for a program called "Scholarships for Latino Kids." I also donated time with Canal Community Alliance, the health van in San Rafael.

Involvement with COTS

When I was volunteering at the library, I was contacted by a COTS member to do volunteer work for them.

So I worked in the COTS kitchen, where I did clean-up and helped prepare meals, chopping vegetables, cleaning potatoes to make mashed potatoes. We had potatoes every Monday, and cleaning hundreds of potatoes was a little boring, but I didn't mind.

The food at COTS is excellent, by the way!

Impressions of COTS Clients

All the people who come to COTS are very nice, and everybody is very responsible. The kids are quiet and sweet. All the clients seem fine about being at COTS and they clearly appreciate the service. One thing that I have learned at COTS is that life can be difficult, but you can get past that difficulty. A lot of people in COTS have done just that, and they are so inspiring.

I met all kinds of people, working in the kitchen. Some people had amazing stories. One person was a very well-known gem cutter. When I was working clean-up he was always coming around helping with clean up and telling me about the jewel business, how the stones were cut. It was very interesting.

This man had become addicted to alcohol and drugs, had lost his job, his wife, his family—everything. He was extremely grateful to COTS for the work that they were doing to help him rehabilitate from his drug and alcohol problems. He also talked about how difficult it was going to be to get back into the business he was in before, cutting gems. He didn't think that he could. But I told him, "You never know what will happen. Keep working on recovering, and one of these days something might fall into your lap that you're not expecting. Because that's the way life usually works. Things fall into your lap that you're not expecting and you go on to a new life. And you say, 'Hey, this'll work out just right.'"

Overcoming Adversity and Unforeseen Physical Challenges

I've always been the kind of person who rises to challenges. Even when someone tells me something is impossible, I try to do it anyway. For example, in 1995 I was rock-climbing and suffered a terrible fall. I was in a coma for three months. I broke both legs, injured one of my eyes, and had a fairly severe brain injury, which affected the portions of the brain that retain memory. As a result, I have almost no memory of my life before 1995, other than photographs and what people tell me. The doctors at the time told me I would never be "normal" again, whatever that means. I had decided on a career in real estate, since physical problems would not allow me to go back to supervising outdoor projects. The doctors said I would never be able to retain enough information for a career like that. But I didn't let that get me down. I took the required classes and passed the real estate test on the first try, which 52% of people fail. I also was able to fix my eye problem without surgery. I did a lot of research, visited specialists, whose techniques I studied and used, and ultimately, through all my work and patience, my eye healed to a degree that allows me normalcy.

Volunteer Philosophy

When people have the energy to give to the community, at some point that energy returns to you. They say that it is through giving that we receive. And I would say from my own experience that I certainly have received more than I've given. I've given a lot, but I've gotten even more back. You always receive by giving; it's the great circle of life.

In life, we must connect with one another. I believe that it's in our nature to be part of something, to commune with others. We all come from the same place and are all part of one another. We're all connected whether we like it or not. Volunteering, which is connecting with people, makes you feel good and useful, which is more important than anything else. It's great karma!

Eric Silverberg

"You don't have to have a five-year plan before you take the first step."

Background

Eric Silverberg began helping COTS when he was in elementary school. He is a recent graduate of Stanford University, worked at Microsoft as a software design engineer, and is presently an MBA candidate at MIT Sloan.

How Eric Found COTS

My family was part of Elim Lutheran Church, which supported COTS in its early, early days, when I was in elementary school. I would help out by collecting food. Then I was re-exposed to COTS in eighth grade through the "Kiss a Cow for COTS" contest that my eighth grade leadership class organized. In ninth grade I started volunteering at COTS. I volunteered with COTS from 1994 up until I left for college in '97.

I worked primarily in the office with the office manager, and everyone else that came through COTS' offices. I met a lot of folks, both employees and a lot of residents too, who would come in and need help. I helped by updating forms and handouts, preparing COTS brochures, and assembling info for Board meetings. I also fielded incoming phone calls.

Later, when the Internet was getting started, we did the first COTS website. We were able to put up some pictures, the mission statement, and simple contact information. Back then, that was pretty high-tech, though not by today's standards. It was one of the first web sites I worked on. I also helped out a little bit with a voice mail system for the shelter, managing that and creating accounts for the residents. My time commitment varied, between two to five hours a week.

I was a freshman at the time I started. There isn't that much for a freshman in high school to do, because you're a little too young to start working but not old enough to be completely swamped with the homework and tests that upperclassmen have. So volunteering my time made sense; it was a great way for me to spend my afternoons doing something helpful and practical.

My work at COTS was really appreciated, and I think that is what kept me coming back throughout my high school years. I felt very valued by the employees of COTS, the volunteers of COTS, and the residents. I didn't feel like I was doing all that much, but people were so grateful and thankful. That made me want to keep coming back, and it seemed like I was making a big difference by doing very simple things.

How Work with COTS Benefited Eric

Serving at COTS benefited me in a couple of ways. It made me a thriftier person—I try to take what I need, and buy only what I know I can use and appreciate.

Beyond that, working at COTS has helped me stay grounded. In the college and professional environments, it's very easy to fall into self-righteous, self-affirming materialistic worldviews. One can easily get caught up in the "reality distortion field" of entitlement. I think my experience with COTS has enabled me to keep a clearer perspective on things, and not to take what I have in life for granted.

Philosophy about Volunteering

I like to do things to surprise myself. Back when I starting volunteering with COTS, it was an unknown quantity. I didn't know what to expect, and didn't know if I'd like it or not. It turned out to be a great experience.

To me, it's good to occasionally make choices that I'm not sure I'm going to like. At the very least, I'm going to be surprised, and that keeps me engaged and having fun. More than that, it keeps me asking questions and sometimes reveals truths that I may have been ignoring or oblivious to.

Thoughts about Service

Service is not something that has to be so big that a person feels completely overwhelmed by it even before they begin. It can be a gradual thing.

A person can even approach service skeptically. And maybe that's a good thing. Go into service and say, "Is this really all it's cracked up to be? Are these organizations really serving people or aren't they?"

You don't have to have a five-year plan before you take the first step. You can just try one day, or try it one hour, and see how it works out. At least you can speak from experience in the future.

I think being involved with COTS has helped my family stay more connected locally. It's a good feeling to have—to invest where you're making a difference, where you're recognized and appreciated. That combination is probably what keeps the Silverbergs coming back.

Jay Silverberg

"The magic comes from doing it."

Background

Jay Silverberg is Eric Silverberg's father. Jay helps COTS with strategic and business planning and media relations. He works with a Washington, DC-based public affairs agency. Jay grew up in south Louisiana as one of five kids and graduated from the University of Missouri with a Bachelor's degree in journalism in 1975. He worked as a reporter and editor for newspapers throughout the US, ending an 18-year newspaper career in 1993, when he began a second career as a media and public relations consultant. Jay and his family have resided in Petaluma since 1986.

Connection to COTS and Service

I've been thinking about my family's connection to COTS, and I will tell you this: It runs in the family. I think of growing up in Thibodaux, Louisiana. Service was something that we did because it was the right thing to do. You never stopped to think about it.

I actually became involved with COTS through my son, Eric. Eric was president of the Petaluma Junior High student body and the school held an annual fundraiser which included a Kiss-A-Cow contest. He asked John Records to kiss a cow, and of course John did, so he got pledges for COTS, and that's the first I truly became aware of John and the work of COTS.

When Eric got to high school, he wanted to do volunteer work. He worked in Diane Landman's office at COTS throughout high school. He built COTS' first web site. Eric once commented that it was his family that got him involved in COTS. If my wife Janet hadn't been taught by her parents that church is important, or I hadn't been taught by my parents that service is important, we wouldn't have passed that along to our kids. Service is something that connects our family, and connects our kids with their grandparents and great grandparents.

I remember my grandmother, my father's mother, owned a grocery store in Kenosha, Wisconsin. Her name was Esther. She had had a woman who worked with her for some 30 odd years. When she decided to retire and move to Louisiana to live with us, she gave the store to this woman. She didn't sell it; she didn't make her buy it. She just gave it to her. She just said, "It's yours."

My grandfather did the same kind of thing in Baton Rouge, Louisiana. We would walk around downtown Baton Rouge, at the time a city of 25 or 30 thousand people, and he always had a quarter to spare for the hobo on the street and everybody knew Mister Buff. And they knew that if they ever needed anything they could always go to him and he would always give it. And that's the way our families were.

And then there's my wife Janet's family. Janet tells stories about her grandmother back in Portland, Oregon when it was a tough town, railroads and the whole bit. She remembers the hobos walking up and down the railroads. Hobos were the homeless of that period. So Janet's grandmother would be baking pies and always hobos were banging on the door, and Janet's grandmother would always have food ready for the people who would come knocking.

So there was never a question that that was the way our family was going to be. Service ran through my entire family in some fashion or form.

I think should Eric get married, or should my daughter Kristen (who has been in the Girl Scouts and continues her relationship with them now that she's in college) get married, that's what they will tell their kids. I think the chances are pretty good that their kids, by natural extension, will step up and help a COTS-like program, help something, help somebody.

It's the threads, it's the connection. And you have to think that if you don't have those threads, then what's the hope, what's the use? At what point do societies cut all those threads and become so disconnected that we never try to help each other?

Nonprofits are one place that people pull the threads together, and work with that connection. And people have to support those nonprofits in any way they can, be it simply by giving them money, giving them product—whatever it might be—or giving them their time. But that's what they have to do. They have to support those nonprofits because the nonprofits are the catch basin for services in a community that by and large bureaucracies just won't do, can't do, can't do as well, or need help doing.

You don't wake up one day and all of a sudden see a light and say, "Okay, today is the day I'm going to serve," but it's a simple thing.

What Keeps You Connected

It's not hard staying connected to this work. One, I enjoy the people, the COTS staff, so much personally. Diane, who manages the family programs, was almost a surrogate mother to Eric when he was volunteering.

Two, it's about helping others who may not be in a position to help themselves at that particular point in their lives. And helping people close to you know what service is; that's service as well. Helping people understand the value. Another word would be outreach.

Three, it's about service. Service in the community, service to an organization, service to COTS. That's what I do. I love doing that type of work. If I could give you a skill or improve on a skill that you already possess so that you can do your job better, I'd love to do that. I did it pro bono when I was with my former employer, and my bosses would make a point of talking to clients about it. We would occasionally get asked if we do pro bono work and they would talk about COTS and they would say, "Our media trainer Jay Silverberg gave training to this organization in Petaluma and we donated the time, the camera and so forth." But to me that was just a natural extension of what service should be. I never stopped to think about that: You needed it, you asked for it and I was only too glad to give it.

The People of COTS

John Records has this interesting manner, a way of making people feel really good about sharing information, and a way of making people feel that they have something unusual or unique to give to COTS. After you talk to him for three or four minutes, you think, "Gosh, I never thought of that aspect of what I do. Gosh, I can really help COTS; I can really do something significant here." He's not working angles, he's not conning people; John just knows how to elicit what people have to offer.

John asked me to be on the Board of COTS, and I came on just when we were deciding whether or not to build the Mary Isaak Center. That was not an easy decision. It was not a unanimous vote; and it was sometimes fairly contentious. We knew that if we did it, we were going to go from this little backwater nonprofit to a major player with people looking at us in ways we'd never been looked at before. We were going to have the state looking at us, grantors looking at us, the city looking at us in a new way, because we were building this grand new glorious homeless shelter. We were going to become a big business overnight, because of the funding that would be required to operate the Isaak Center.

Some people felt it was a mistake. COTS shouldn't do this, we shouldn't grow, we shouldn't take on this burden! We knew we'd better start figuring out how to raise money in a real serious way. Roger Kirkpatrick came to us and said, "I'll help you figure it out." He had managed major corporations. He's this unusual man who came into our lives and adopted COTS and thank God he did. He did his research, and he found a method that was being offered to nonprofits that would help us raise serious funds and build an endowment. Since then we've raised close to a million dollars.

Then there's Don Louvier, who works at our community Kitchen. He has this way about him that is at once moving and honorable and heartbreaking when you hear him talk about twenty-odd years ago, losing the love of his life, his wife. He didn't understand why the only person he had ever loved had been taken from him; he felt it was unfair. He spiraled down, he lost everything, and for ten to fifteen years he lived on the streets of Petaluma. People saw him, but they didn't SEE him. Now you can't miss him.

I see homeless people completely differently now. I don't just see them, I SEE them, I notice them. I look at them. And I think: "There's life there. It's gone terribly awry. How did it happen? What is the world doing to help that person?"

At times, I try offer to buy them something to eat, or a cup of coffee. If you can at least get that few minutes of their time and attention—because they will give it to you—they will listen a little bit, and then you can ask, Do you have the time to go to the Salvation Army? Do you have the time to go to COTS? Do you know what COTS is? That's what John, and Diane, and Mike Johnson and Roger and Don and many others have taught me.

Service to COTS and Its Impact on My Life

I know I am a lot better at what I do when I have to counsel with corporations, because I listen better, and I think better, because of what I've seen and learned through my contact with COTS.

When clients come to my firm it's not too dissimilar to someone coming to Don or John and saying, "I'm at my wits end, I lost my job six months ago, I haven't been to an AA meeting in a week," and so forth.

You have to listen, and you can't panic, and you have to be dispassionate, and you have to be loving, and you have to be giving. You also have to be pretty forceful about it—at COTS we have to tell people, "You have to get your life together. You're in a very hard situation, you'll have to make some hard choices and you'll have tough consequences if you don't follow through, but we're going to help you as much as we can." It's the same thing, professionally, in my line of work.

Advice for Others on Service

I do think some people believe for whatever reason that service, volunteering has to be this overwhelming, overpowering "Oh my God, if I
don't give them $5,000 I am not giving enough" kind of experience. But
that's not it at all. It's just making the effort, whatever it is. And once you
start, you begin to decide, "Well, that's kind of interesting," and then you
take another step and another and another.

It's easy. There is no magic to it. The magic comes from doing it. Just
take the step and go. If you're not a member of a congregation, that's fine. If
you are not religious, that's fine. If you decide to donate to United Way or
want to give your money to the Susan G. Komen Foundation, that's service.
Because it might help somebody. Who knows? You may be the one who
helps find the cure to breast cancer. Just take the step. It's just simple.
You've just got to do it.

Jim Winkel

"If I have something I can offer,
why wouldn't I do it? . . . No matter what
you give, you get so much more back."

Background

Jim Winkel was raised and educated in Sheboygan, Wisconsin, but spent part of his childhood in Springfield, Massachusetts. He met his wife in Wisconsin, and moved to California thirty years ago. He got involved with computers during his college years when he joined the Air Force. When he arrived in California, he worked at Honeywell and then General Electric. After fifteen years in the high tech corporate world, Jim decided to become a small business owner. He sold restaurant equipment, and owned a gourmet food store, and a restaurant in the South Bay until 1998 when he moved to Petaluma. Jim is currently self-employed, as a designer of restaurants.

Along with his involvement with COTS, Jim has been an active volunteer in other Petaluma organizations, including the Lion's Club, Rebuilding Together, and the Healthy Community Consortium. He also supports PEP, Petaluma Ecumenical Properties.

Early Influences on Thoughts about Charity

My dad was one of the most giving, generous people that I've ever known. My father just believes that if you have something, you share it. I think a lot of that was the Midwestern upbringing that my father had. He didn't ever talk about it; he just did it and taught me by example.

I always have had a problem saying no, particularly to people who have less than I do. And in many cases I *shouldn't* say no. An example is the COTS Kitchen—if I have something I can offer, why wouldn't I do it? It's kind of inconceivable for me to *not do it.*

What Brought Jim into Contact with COTS

I frequently end up with used equipment after re-designing a kitchen that doesn't have a high resale value, and the value of these used items to the COTS Kitchen is dramatic. So John Sedlander came into our office, looking for some things for the COTS facility. I went through our used items, and also figured out how I could help them cut costs, since I had experience with designing kitchens.

The COTS Kitchen was something I could make an immediate contribution to—it's not the same as trying to find a home for orphans or housing for single mothers, which I think is a tremendous thing to do, but I couldn't do it. But because of my business, I can influence the COTS Kitchen in a positive way—many times by just going out to the warehouse and taking something down.

Stories about Volunteering and Lessons Learned

I was standing in the parking lot at the Opportunity Center, and I was dropping something off, and here comes a woman who looked very pretty and fairly well-dressed, walking maybe a hundred feet away from us. I was thinking, "Man, this woman is kind of brave, and a little out of place." She came closer, and then I could see that she was just ravaged. Her face was hollow and there were pock-marks. It just hits you: from a distance, you never would have known her story or how incorrect your first impression was.

Here is another one that I won't forget. John Sedlander and I were having a little meeting at COTS, setting up the kitchen area, and this punk, Goth-style young lady came in. I would guess that she was in her early twenties. She was wearing black tattered but not dirty clothes—with this alternative-lifestyle kind of look. I was thinking to myself that it was a shame that someone this young was out in the streets. And she walks up and she says, "Do you have anything for me to do in here, John, or should I go outside?" She was one of the volunteers! I finished up my business, walked out to my car, and here was this young gal surrounded by three or four much older clients in their forties and fifties. They were all sitting down, and the obvious respect that they showed her while she was talking to them made me feel like such a judgmental fool. Thank God no one else knew how much of a fool I was. Here was this young, young person sharing her personality and offering a type of emotional support to these people. She just went out and talked to these guys. Not only did she have no fear; they just looked at her like Mother Theresa. It was amazing. I drove away thinking about how grateful I was that I didn't say anything stupid.

Maybe that's the beauty of wisdom—it doesn't come overnight. And it's not just a "Don't judge a book by its cover" sort of lesson to me. It's the idea that we all give what we can, and this young lady was obviously giving some degree of comfort to these people.

What Service Means to Jim

If you haven't figured this out yet through your own experience, then I would tell you that no matter what you give--you get so much more back. People hear this all the time from people that are involved with volunteering, and it is an absolute fact. If you give an hour, you get days of satisfaction. I have never had a situation where I haven't felt blessed by what I got for what little I gave.

What I get back is so personal—I don't have any ability to express it. Just the simple act of giving, the time that you spend, *feels* great. Hopefully you get back things like a little better understanding, and a little more tolerance of people, the little life lessons. But in general, you just feel good about what you do.

Unfortunately, as the years go by, the percentage of people who are able and willing to help seems to go down. I think there's maybe 20% of the population, or some number in that range, that will always be the ones that get things done. I think 80% of people would rather get in their campers on weekends. And I don't blame them; that's their personal call. I think you can look along the streets and say, "Most of these people are never going to get involved." But that's okay. Take the ones that will.

OVERVIEW OF COTS PROGRAMS

COTS provides a comprehensive range of award-winning programs and support services designed to help children, families, and adults break the cycle of homelessness.

COTS offers nearly 300 beds each night, and serves about 100,000 free meals each year.

COTS volunteers donate approximately 50,000 hours annually.

Children

Our Center For Homeless Children and Their Families has a licensed day care program located on-site to provide safe care, tutoring, and assessment for children while their parents go to work or find work.

At the core of our family programs is *Kids First*, a 12-week course on parenting skills. Topics include stages of child development, nurturing self-esteem in children, and positive discipline.

Families

COTS serves families through our emergency shelter program at the Center for Homeless Children and Their Families, through our Faith Based Shelter, and through our Shared and Transitional Housing.

We teach budgeting, life skills, and parenting classes and we provide case management and counseling to prepare families for a home of their own.

Rent Right, a nine-week course that prepares parents to transition to independent housing, teaches budgeting, credit repair, housing applications, home maintenance, and more.

Adults

COTS' residential shelter, the Mary Isaak Center, each year serves approximately 770 homeless adults who do not have children in their care. With a foundation of rigorous drug testing and strict rules ("no chore, no bed") the Isaak Center helps chronically homeless adults rebuild their lives.

Work Right, our job skills training program, provides case management, counseling, and help with goal setting and building self-esteem, as well as transferable job skills.

Meals

Our Petaluma Kitchen serves more than 80,000 free hot meals per year, and our Food for Families program delivers more than 250,000 pounds of food each year as free weekly food boxes for low-income seniors and families in Petaluma.

Much of the food is donated from food drives and local merchants.

For more information about COTS programs, volunteer information, and other ways to support COTS, please visit the COTS website at **www.cots-homeless.org**

www.ingramcontent.com/pod-product-compliance
Lightning Source LLC
Chambersburg PA
CBHW031202270326
41931CB00006B/369